MW00782640

BUILDING YOUR BUILDING

How to Hire and KEEP Great Teachers

JASMINE K. KULLAR • SCOTT A. CUNNINGHAM

FOREWORD BY MIKE MATTOS

Solution Tree | Press

a division of
Solution Tree

Copyright © 2020 by Solution Tree Press

Materials appearing here are copyrighted. With one exception, all rights are reserved. Readers may reproduce only those pages marked "Reproducible." Otherwise, no part of this book may be reproduced or transmitted in any form or by any means (electronic, photocopying, record-ing, or otherwise) without prior written permission of the publisher.

555 North Morton Street
Bloomington, IN 47404
800.733.6786 (toll free) / 812.336.7700
FAX: 812.336.7790

email: info@SolutionTree.com
SolutionTree.com

Visit **go.SolutionTree.com/leadership** to download the free reproducibles in this book.

Printed in the United States of America

Library of Congress Cataloging-in-Publication Data

Names: Kullar, Jasmine K., 1976- author. | Cunningham, Scott A., 1971- author.
Title: Building your building : how to hire and keep great teachers /
   authors, Jasmine K. Kullar and Scott A. Cunningham.
Description: Bloomington, IN : Solution Tree Press, [2020] | Includes
   bibliographical references and index.
Identifiers: LCCN 2019002631 | ISBN 9781947604810 (perfect bound)
Subjects: LCSH: Teachers--Recruiting--United States. | Teachers--Selection
   and appointment--United States. | First year teachers--Training of--United States.
Classification: LCC LB2835.25 .K85 2020 | DDC 370.71/1--dc23 LC record available at
https://lccn.loc.gov/2019002631

Solution Tree
Jeffrey C. Jones, CEO
Edmund M. Ackerman, President

Solution Tree Press
President and Publisher: Douglas M. Rife
Associate Publisher: Sarah Payne-Mills
Art Director: Rian Anderson
Managing Production Editor: Kendra Slayton
Senior Production Editor: Suzanne Kraszewski
Senior Editor: Amy Rubenstein
Copy Editor: Evie Madsen
Proofreader: Sarah Ludwig
Cover Designer: Abigail Bowen
Editorial Assistant: Sarah Ludwig

Acknowledgments

Thank you, Mom and Dad, for being my biggest cheerleaders and for always being there. I wouldn't be where I am if it wasn't for your constant support and faith. Thank you to my brother, Paul; your unconditional love and support has meant the world to me. Thank you to my in-laws for always being proud of me. Thank you to my husband, Balraj; without your constant encouragement, love, and patience, I couldn't have done any of this. Lastly, thank you to my daughter, Sabrina, and my son, Dillon. You both are my inspiration for everything!

—Jasmine Kullar

I would like to thank my son, Ty, who inspires so many of my stories because he always makes me laugh and is one of the most incredible humans on earth. I love you, buddy. I would also like to thank my wife, Bay, who is the most incredible person in the world. You inspire me every day. I know that when you were born the world became a better place, and the day I met you I became a better man.

—Scott Cunningham

We both would like to thank our Solution Tree family for all of their help and support through this process, especially Jeff Jones for his never-ending commitment to making kids' lives better through every book he publishes. Your leadership is incredibly valued and appreciated. Thank you to Claudia Wheatley for facilitating our collaboration and continuously pushing us out of our comfort zones. Thank you to the amazing editorial and marketing teams at Solution Tree; you were instrumental in making this book happen, and we are so grateful!

We will always be thankful to Rick and Becky DuFour and Bob Eaker for all of their wit and wisdom that guided our path to this book.

Solution Tree Press would like to thank the following reviewers:

Paul Gebel
Principal
Denver Secondary School
Denver, Iowa

Brian Hoelscher
Principal
Central Intermediate School
Washington, Illinois

Jonathan Howell
Principal
Fossil Ridge Intermediate School
Saint George, Utah

Craig Mah
Principal
Walton Elementary School
Coquitlam, British Columbia
Canada

Ann Rutherford
Assistant Principal
Daniel J. Bakie Elementary School
Kingston, New Hampshire

Visit **go.SolutionTree.com/leadership** to download the free reproducibles in this book.

Table of Contents

Reproducible pages are in italics.

PART 1: HIRING GREAT TEACHERS

PART 2: KEEPING GREAT TEACHERS

3   Supporting New Teachers **63**

4   Mentoring New Teachers **93**

5   Recognizing Teachers **113**

6 Implementing Professional Development 137

About the Authors

Jasmine K. Kullar, EdD, is an assistant superintendent for Cobb County School District, the second-largest school district in Georgia. She is also a faculty member in the College of Professional Studies Educational Leadership Department at Albany State University in Georgia.

Prior to these roles, Jasmine was a middle school principal for seven years at two separate schools. With over ten years of school leadership experience, Jasmine has worked at the elementary, middle, and high school levels. She has taught in both Canada and the United States, giving her a variety of experiences in working with schools and school districts. She has expertise in the professional learning community (PLC) process as well as with school leadership.

Scott A. Cunningham is principal of Orange Middle School (Olentangy Local School District) in Ohio. He has over twenty-three years of experience in education as a principal, an assistant principal, and a teacher.

As principal of Norton Middle School in Columbus, Ohio, Scott and his team transformed this low-achieving school into a nationally recognized model PLC. With a poverty rate of over 75 percent and a diverse population of students from over twenty countries, Norton earned an excellent rating from the Ohio Department of Education, making adequate yearly progress in all areas and demonstrating above-average growth in value-added data (top 15 percent in the state).

He holds a bachelor's degree in biology from Ohio Northern University and a master's in curriculum and instruction from Ashland University.

To book Jasmine K. Kullar and Scott A. Cunningham for professional development, contact pd@SolutionTree.com.

Foreword

by Mike Mattos

So you are responsible for hiring new faculty members in your school or district; congratulations—what a daunting responsibility! The positions you are hiring for require not only a prerequisite level of professional training, but also strong interpersonal skills and high moral character. To be great, new hires should possess the wisdom of a judge, the empathy of a counselor, the diplomacy of an ambassador, the dedication of a missionary, and the perseverance of a marathon runner. By the third year of employment, they will most likely gain tenure, making it virtually impossible to remove them from your team. This decision will cost your school and district thousands of dollars in the short term, and potentially millions over the teacher's career. And, most importantly, whomever you select will be trusted with the most cherished individuals in our society: children. The success—or failure—of the people you hire will impact generations of families in your community.

With so much at stake, surely educational leaders use a proven process to recruit, hire, and nurture new faculty. When leaders enter the profession, they probably experience carefully designed supports to ensure their success. Unfortunately, this is not often the case.

I vividly remember my first year of teaching. It was 1987, and I had recently graduated from the University of Redlands in California with a degree in political science. During my last semester, one of my student-teaching assignments was at a local junior high school. Fortunately, the principal saw some potential in me and offered me a position for the coming school year. I was one of three new teachers that fall.

My preliminary credential qualified me to teach secondary social science. Unfortunately, the principal did not have enough history sections to fill my schedule, so I was asked to also teach two pre-algebra classes. Needless to say, none of my assigned course titles started with the word *honors*, *accelerated*, or *gifted*. Because I took only one mathematics course in college, I had to apply for an emergency credential and agree to earn at least eight collegiate mathematics credits during the school year. Additionally, the State of California gave new teachers up to five years to complete additional units of study to transition from a preliminary to a clear credential. This meant that three nights a week—from six to nine in the evening—I took mathematics and history classes at a local community college.

Unfortunately, the school where I was teaching did not have enough classrooms, so I taught two history classes in room G8, then walked across campus to teach my two mathematics classes in the metal shop room, and then came back to G8 for a third history class. There were no student desks in the metal shop room, only large wooden tables students sat around, eight to a station. The veteran teachers with classrooms in the G wing were notorious jokesters. When I arrived the morning of the first day for students, the drawers of my desk were pulled out, the contents dumped across the top of my desk, and a note perched atop the mess that demanded, "Bring cookies!"

There were no state standards in California at that time, so I was given a teacher's edition of the textbook for each course. That was it. Luckily, a veteran mathematics teacher—Wally Powell—was kind enough to share with me a copy of his weekly test that he gave on Fridays. This provided me with some idea of what to teach each week. I created every lesson from scratch. That year, I also served as the school's assistant yearbook advisor and assistant girls' volleyball coach. In January, my landlord unexpectedly raised our rent. My wife and I could not afford the increase, so we moved fifteen miles farther away from the school, to a much less desirable neighborhood. Somehow I survived that first year—a true trial by fire. But one of the other new teachers who started the same time as I did decided to leave the profession—forever.

I do not share this story to sound like an old-timer pining about how hard we had it back then. (No, I did not walk to school barefoot and uphill both ways!) The point is that I don't think my experience is rare, but instead the norm in education. If our goal should be to successfully hire, develop, and support new faculty members, it would be hard to design a process that would have made my first year *more* difficult. Of course my principal did not purposely try to make my first year exceedingly hard; she was merely perpetuating traditional practices. Ask any gathering of teachers who is most likely to get assigned the most difficult classes in the school, and they will unanimously shout, "The new hires!" These practices are not only common, but almost universally expected and accepted.

Few organizations, businesses, and professions would survive the loss of so many new hires as in the field of education. In the past, schools usually had more applicants than teaching openings. So when one teacher left, a new recruit was ready and willing to join the fray. But as the authors of this book show, today many districts and states are facing severe teacher shortages, with fewer college students deciding to join the ranks. These shortages often place substitute or insufficiently trained teachers in service of the most at-risk students. While there are many factors that contribute to the high teacher attrition rate, undoubtedly much of the damage is self-inflicted.

If we—as professional educators—are going to achieve our collective mission of ensuring high levels of learning for every student, then we must rethink and redesign the way we attract, recruit, hire, assign, and support our colleagues. That is the purpose of this book!

Jasmine Kullar and Scott Cunningham have filled every chapter with research-based ideas and real-life examples. Specifically, the authors advocate that schools function as a professional learning community (PLC) to best meet the needs of educators and students. PLCs operate under the assumption that the key to improved learning for students is continuous job-embedded learning for educators. Therefore, purposeful structures ensure staff members engage in job-embedded learning as part of their routine work practices (DuFour, DuFour, Eaker, Many, & Mattos, 2016). Such practices benefit both new and veteran teachers.

I have had the privilege of working with Jasmine and Scott. They are award-winning educators, having led nationally-recognized model PLCs. Their recommendations are not theory, but proven practices that they utilized and perfected at their own schools and districts. After reading this book, my first thought was, "I wish this book was available when I was a site principal."

Undoubtedly, implementing these recommendations will require some courageous leadership. Change is difficult, especially when challenging traditional practices that have disproportionately benefited the most veteran teachers on each campus. The spoils of seniority cannot come at the cost of new staff and student learning. For in the end, we are not initiating a new pledge class into a college fraternity, but welcoming new colleagues into an honorable profession.

Introduction: Million-Dollar Decisions

Have you ever been responsible for making a *million-dollar decision*? These are critical, high-stakes decisions that have the potential to elevate your organization to star status or sink it into obscurity. You may think you haven't, but if you are a school leader, you most definitely have made many high-risk decisions. Consider, for example, the decisions you make when hiring a new teacher.

When hiring a new teacher, you aren't simply hiring a person who will instruct students; you are hiring a person who will impact student lives—a person who may be the only adult a student can relate to, or the person who may end up saving a student's life. You are hiring a person who will open up new worlds for students. He or she can dramatically impact a student's life for the better. This is no small task. Making the wrong choice can have profound consequences. So when you hire a teacher, you are making a million-dollar decision.

So how do school leaders know how to make the right decision? How can you be sure to hire the right person for the job? And even more important, how do you ensure you keep the great teachers you hire? How do you build the best building possible? First, let's look at the climate of the teaching profession.

A Teacher Supply Problem

During the 2015–2016 school year, there were over 330 articles written about teacher shortages while only 24 articles were written about this topic two years prior (Sutcher, Darling-Hammond, & Carver-Thomas, 2016). Not only is the pool of teachers declining, but the number of people pursuing teaching careers has also declined (Sutcher et al., 2016). Specifically, teachers enrolled in teacher preparation programs is down 35 percent, and the percentage of graduates from teacher preparation programs has decreased 23 percent (Sutcher et al., 2016). In addition,

Leib Sutcher, Linda Darling-Hammond, and Desiree Carver-Thomas (2016) predicted there will be a 20 percent increase in teacher demand by 2025 because of the following factors.

- Student enrollment will grow by three million due to immigration and higher birth rates.

- Students-to-teacher ratios will decrease, which could require an additional 145,000 teachers by 2025.

- Teacher attrition is high; two-thirds of teachers who leave the profession do so before retirement because of job dissatisfaction.

In fact, when looking at teacher attrition rates, the National Center for Education Statistics (NCES; Gray & Taie, 2015) provided the following information over a five-year period (from 2007 to 2011).

- Among all beginning teachers in 2007–2008, 10 percent did not teach in 2008–2009, 12 percent did not teach in 2009–2010, 15 percent did not teach in 2010–2011, and 17 percent did not teach in 2011–2012.

- During their second year (in 2008–2009), 74 percent of beginning teachers taught in the same school as the previous year (called the *stayers*), 16 percent taught in a different school (the *movers*), and 10 percent were not teaching.

- During their fifth year (in 2011–2012), 70 percent of beginning teachers taught in the same school as the previous year (stayers), 10 percent taught in a different school (movers), 3 percent had returned to teaching after not teaching the previous year (the *returners*), and 17 percent were not teaching.

We have a teacher supply problem with fewer teachers entering the profession coupled with an increase in students entering schools (Darling-Hammond, 2003; Sutcher et al., 2016; Gray & Taie, 2015). "Since the early 1990s, the annual number of exits from teaching has surpassed the number of entrants by an increasingly large amount . . . for example, while U.S. schools hired 230,000 teachers in 1999, 287,000 left in that year" (Darling-Hammond, 2003, p. 7). Therefore, the need for teachers is increasing, but the teachers are leaving. This is why both hiring and retaining teachers are significant issues in education.

We know the devastating impact on schools and students when teachers leave and principals are faced with the task of hiring all over again. The National Commission on Teaching and America's Future (2007) finds the financial cost associated with hiring and training as a result of teacher turnover is almost $7.3 billion per year. One might suggest that if we just raised teacher salaries, this problem of turnover and low supply would go away. Unfortunately, principals and most school leaders do not control salary as a way to entice teachers to stay; however, they can control how they lead the school, which has a significant impact on hiring and keeping teachers.

The Need for Solid Leadership

An *Education Week* survey of five hundred teachers finds that leadership is more important than salary when it comes to teachers staying in their jobs (Viadero, 2018). Educators Richard DuFour, Rebecca DuFour, Robert Eaker, Thomas W. Many, and Mike Mattos (2016) state, "When teachers have positive perceptions about their work environment, their principals, and the cohesion and support of their colleagues, they are more likely to remain in their schools because of their high levels of satisfaction with their work" (p. 202). Authors Sarah Almy and Melissa Tooley (2012) find that the following factors have more impact on teacher retention than salaries: when principals create a culture that includes collaboration, a commitment to using data to drive instructional decisions, and strong leadership.

Since principals can't control every aspect of the educational environment, they must focus on the factors they can control to create the best environment for students. One of the factors principals can control is the culture they create in their buildings. Are you leading a school with a culture that is conducive to attracting teachers and then retaining them? Have you created an environment with a relentless focus on learning, where every policy, practice, and decision is based on what is best for student learning? Have you created a collaborative culture with teacher teams collaborating about the *right* work? Have you created a results-oriented environment where teacher teams analyze student data and make instructional decisions based on that data? These characteristics describe a professional learning community (PLC; DuFour et al., 2016).

We believe implementing the PLC process to create such a culture is a school's best chance for building the foundation necessary to hire the right teachers and retain them. In a PLC, teachers are not alone as they collaborate, learn from each other, celebrate together, and problem solve with one another, creating a culture of interdependence in which the focus is on student results. Imagine hiring new teachers into such a culture; in a PLC, they immediately have the support they need. If you would like to learn more about how to become a PLC, we recommend the following books:

- *Learning by Doing, Third Edition*, by Richard DuFour, Rebecca DuFour, Robert Eaker, Thomas W. Many, and Mike Mattos
- *Kid by Kid, Skill by Skill* by Robert Eaker and Janel Keating
- *Cultures Built to Last* by Richard DuFour and Michael Fullan
- *The Five Disciplines of PLC Leaders* by Timothy D. Kanold
- *Leaders of Learning* by Richard DuFour and Robert J. Marzano
- *Leading by Design* by Cassandra Erkens and Eric Twadell
- *Making Teamwork Meaningful* by William M. Ferriter, Parry Graham, and Matt Wight

About This Book

This book is for any school leader who is responsible for hiring and leading teachers. That can be school principals, assistant principals, or teacher leaders. We strongly recommend this book to district leaders as well so they can provide the right support and tools to help their schools hire and retain teachers.

The book has two parts. The first part (chapters 1 and 2) focuses on hiring, and the second part (chapters 3 to 6) focuses on keeping great teachers.

- Chapter 1 helps school leaders consider what it means to be an effective teacher by outlining the features of effective teachers. It answers the question, What makes a teacher great? We believe before they can hope to hire and retain great teachers in their schools, leaders must be crystal clear on the features of effective teachers.

- Chapter 2 outlines practices for hiring effective teachers, including marketing, promoting upward mobility, utilizing college partnerships, recruiting, reviewing applications and résumés, interviewing (and alternatives), questioning, spotting untruthful candidates, and doing reference checks.

- Chapter 3 looks at the important responsibility of supporting new teachers. This chapter describes the different types of support for new teachers and practical strategies for school leaders to provide that support.

- Chapter 4 focuses on mentoring new teachers, describing different ways to mentor new teachers, and defining the mentor's role. We offer strategies to help make your mentoring program effective for new teachers.

- Chapter 5 looks at the task of recognizing new teachers and why recognition is so important in helping retain teachers. We examine characteristics of effective recognition programs and discuss why many leaders find it difficult to recognize teachers. We then offer practical strategies that can help leaders begin recognizing teachers.

- Chapter 6 examines professional development for new teachers. We discuss what makes professional development effective versus ineffective and offer strategies to help school leaders create a professional development program for new teachers that will help them be successful.

At the end of every chapter, we include a Next Steps section that describes that chapter's reproducible tools to aid leaders as they begin applying the material. Each chapter also includes Reflection Questions school leaders can use to self-reflect or facilitate a group discussion among a group of school leaders.

Look Ahead

As you read through this book, you will learn strategies and find tools to help you hire the best teachers and not only retain those new teachers you hire but hopefully retain all your teachers. Take the time to engage in the reflection questions at the end of every chapter to self-reflect on your new learning and use the reproducibles to help you get the best for your students, your school, and your district.

PART I

HIRING GREAT TEACHERS

CHAPTER 1

Features of Effective Teachers

Choose a job you love and you will never have to work a day in your life.

—Confucius

If we agree that hiring great teachers is critical for school leaders—perhaps the most critical decision they make—we must first understand what makes a great teacher. Sometimes principals and other school leaders engage in all the right processes, but still end up making the wrong decision. How can this happen? We propose that often school leaders lack a clear picture of what they desire. They lack a clear vision of the stakes of their million-dollar decision. Before embarking on the task of hiring, school leaders must understand what it is to be a great teacher. To make the right decision, you first need to know what the right decision looks like.

In this chapter, we shine a spotlight on what it means to be a great teacher, specifically the idea of being effective. We outline the features of effective teachers, both the characteristics effective teachers have and the processes they engage in, and we provide reproducibles for leaders to use when clarifying their thoughts about and reflecting on their expectations of effective teachers.

Great Teachers Are Effective

Now take a moment to think about a great teacher in your school. What makes this teacher great? Take a few minutes to jot down those features. Chances are you have written several features tied either to the teacher's personality or the way he or she teaches.

The *Merriam-Webster Dictionary* defines great as being "remarkable in magnitude, degree, or effectiveness"; "remarkably skilled"; or "markedly superior in character or quality" ("Great," n.d.). When you have a great teacher who exhibits certain traits that makes him or her remarkably skilled or superior in quality, then that is a teacher who is effective. That is a teacher who is making an impact on student achievement, a teacher who is making a difference.

In order to have an understanding of what makes teachers effective, we want to first differentiate between *characteristics* of the teacher and the *processes* the teacher uses to ensure all students learn.

Characteristics of Effective Teachers

Characteristics are those features that teachers just have or don't have. These characteristics are hard to teach and hard to instill, but not impossible. The following are four characteristics of effective teachers.

1. Passion

2. A caring nature

3. High expectations

4. Capacity for reflection

Passion

Effective teachers are passionate about their content and their students, and for learning. They love what they teach, and they love the challenge of making sure all students learn; and, above all, they love their students. Their passion is contagious as they infect their students with their love of learning (Hattie, 2009).

It's often easy to spot teachers who have lost their passion. They might make excuses for why their students are not learning or why they themselves have no need to learn or try anything new. Or they might openly make negative comments about their students. Most school leaders have heard statements such as, "I can't stand this kid!" or "These kids are awful!" A teacher might exclaim, "Why do I need to go to this training?" We have seen through our combined years of work with teachers that when teachers lose their passion, their effectiveness decreases. Unfortunately, students perceive when teachers do not like them, when teachers don't care if they are learning, and when teachers have no interest in their own professional growth. School leaders need to avoid such negative energy at all costs.

Conversely, effective teachers maintain their passion every day for every student they teach as well as for their own profession by dedicating themselves to being life-long learners. Education researcher Hamdi Serin (2017) finds, "passionate teachers work with enthusiasm, constantly increase their devotion and commitment and they believe in the importance of their job" (p. 61). Importantly, passionate teachers meet their students' needs by continuing to learn and grow as teachers, becoming the best teachers they can be. As a result, passionate teachers involve themselves in various kinds of professional learning opportunities such as attending workshops, reading articles or books, or observing others teaching.

A Caring Nature

Effective teachers respect their students as learners and treat students as if they are their own children. We all want our own children to have incredible lives and experiences, and the most effective teachers take this approach with their students. Russell A. Barkley, author, clinical psychologist, and professor of psychiatry, states, "The children who need love the most will always ask for it in the most unloving ways." Effective teachers understand this and make sure they take care of *all* students—even those who are the toughest to love.

Students often bring so much baggage into the classroom that sometimes teachers must meet their basic needs before learning can take place. Psychologist Abraham H. Maslow (1943), in his hierarchy of needs theory, states humans have five basic needs that must be met in order for them to be motivated and satisfied: (1) psychological, (2) safety, (3) love and belonging, (4) esteem and accomplishment, and (5) self-actualization. *Care* relates specifically to the first level of physiological needs, which includes needs such as hunger (Maslow, 1943). Caring teachers understand that meeting such needs is part of being effective. Think about the teacher who always has snacks in his or her classroom in case a student is hungry, or the teacher who takes the time to talk to a student privately (so as not to embarrass him or her in front of peers) to see if he or she has a warm enough coat. Teachers who genuinely care about their students are more focused on seeing them as children who need guidance and structure, rather than seeing them as automatons who must do what is asked of them at all times, regardless of what they may be going through psychologically.

One of the top reasons young people identify for dropping out of school is they felt nobody in the school cared about them (Doll, Eslami, & Walters, 2013). We know the terrible ramifications of dropping out—everything from lower wages, lower quality of life, higher rates of incarceration, and shorter life spans. The Alliance for Excellent Education (2014) shares the following statistics in their report, *The High Cost of High School Dropouts: The Economic Case for Reducing the High School Dropout Rate.*

- High school dropouts are three times more likely to be unemployed than college graduates.

- High school dropouts who are employed make $8,000 less per year than high school graduates and $26,500 less per year than college graduates.

- Sixty-seven percent of inmates in America's state prisons are high school dropouts.

- Because high school dropouts are generally less healthy, the United States could save $7.3 billion in annual Medicaid spending if the high school dropout rate decreased by half.

If we know one of the top reasons students identify for dropping out is feeling as though nobody at school cares for them, then it is critical for school leaders to seek, hire, and keep effective teachers who truly care about students.

High Expectations

Effective teachers have high expectations for their students, and effective teachers believe in their ability to help all students learn and grow no matter what baggage students might bring to the classroom. Researcher John A. C. Hattie (2003) suggests that habitually challenging students to improve and grow is one the most important factors separating great teachers from the rest of the pack. Many teachers may argue that they have high expectations, but unfortunately, sometimes what they consider high expectations is really just an excuse for them to be difficult, hard, or mean. Having high expectations is when a teacher believes students can rise to meet expectations (both behavioral and academic), so the teacher supports the students and scaffolds learning until students reach those expectations.

Effective teachers keep trying different strategies and different techniques until students get it. Of course, this is much easier and effective to do in a PLC. In PLCs, educators believe all students can learn at high levels, and PLC processes ensure students meet high expectations (DuFour et al., 2016). For example, the three big ideas of a PLC—(1) a focus on learning, (2) a collaborative culture and collective responsibility, and (3) a results orientation—all support educators in their quest for higher and higher student achievement. When teachers collaborate together in a PLC, they determine not only what that high level of expectation is for learning, but also what they will do when students do not master it. In a PLC, teachers in their collaborative teams do whatever it takes to ensure every student they teach will rise to that expectation.

Capacity for Reflection

Effective teachers always seek to improve. They take opportunities to reflect on, analyze, and refine their processes to improve or change to achieve better outcomes. Effective teachers do not become defensive. They do not make excuses. They do not believe the problem lies with others. Educator and author Beth Lewis (n.d.) states,

> In a profession as challenging as teaching, honest self-reflection is key. That means that we must regularly examine what has worked and what hasn't worked in the classroom, despite how painful it can sometimes be to look in the mirror.

Being reflective requires being open to change. Consider the following scenario.

A collaborative team is analyzing its test data. One teacher realizes he has more failing students than anyone else on the team. If he is ineffective, that teacher will begin listing excuses: "I have all the low-performing students" or "My students this year are so lazy." If this teacher is an effective teacher, he immediately reflects on how he taught the material and on what he needs to do differently, and then takes steps to improve his practice. In a PLC, collaborative teams of teachers follow a cycle of continuous improvement that involves data collection about effectiveness, followed by reflection and collaboration on how to revise and improve (DuFour et al., 2016). Reflective teachers also feel responsible when their students do not learn; they take it personally. This is true of collaborative teams in PLCs as well, where there is a culture of *our students* rather than *your students versus my students* (DuFour et al., 2016).

The reproducible "Planning Template to Strengthen the Four Characteristics" (pages 23–24) provides some strategies to strengthen these characteristics so you have more teachers who exhibit these traits in your school or district. This reproducible also offers space for you to brainstorm some of your own strategies that you can try as well. The purpose is to hire and keep teachers who continuously exhibit passion, a caring nature, high expectations, and a capacity for reflection. The second feature of effective teachers is their use of effective processes. This is perhaps a more concrete and measurable feature.

Effective Teacher Processes

Characteristics are the *what*, while processes are the *how*. Characteristics are those specific features that make teachers effective. Processes, on the other hand, are how teachers do their jobs that makes them either effective or ineffective.

In *Visible Learning for Teachers: Maximizing Impact on Learning*, Hattie (2012) shares the following five processes that he finds highly effective teachers employ.

1. Achieving clarity

2. Facilitating classroom discussion

3. Using formative assessment

4. Implementing metacognitive strategies

5. Collaborating with colleagues

Building your building with teachers who are strong in these particular processes is critical. These are the practices teachers need to implement while doing their jobs in order to be effective. These processes are those duties and responsibilities of the teaching job that, if done well, can make a significant impact on student achievement. The reproducible "Assessment of Teaching Practices" (page 25) is a rubric you can utilize to help evaluate how many of your teachers use these practices.

Achieving Clarity

Educational researcher and author Mike Schmoker (2003) notes, "Clarity precedes competence." Likewise, the architects of the PLC at Work process, Richard DuFour and Robert Eaker, and PLC visionary Rebecca DuFour, when describing the foundations of the PLC process—mission, vision, values (collective commitments), and goals—stress that schools must be crystal clear about what they are, what they want to become, what their commitments to each other are to get there, and what their goals are (DuFour et al., 2016).

If your school or district is not functioning as a PLC, leaders can help teachers achieve clarity by ensuring teachers know and understand their curriculum and standards. Are they able to unpack the standards to identify the learning targets in each standard? Are teachers able to clearly connect the standards to the assessments they write? Can teachers clearly articulate what success looks like to their students? Of course, in a PLC, this process is much more effective because all of this is done in collaboration with other teachers.

In a PLC, achieving clarity connects directly to the four critical questions of a PLC (DuFour et al., 2016). Effective teachers work within their collaborative teams to become crystal clear about the answers to the following questions.

1. **What do we want students to know and be able to do?** Effective teachers use standards and work with colleagues to determine the *essential learnings*—what they want students to learn. Once they do this, they clarify these expectations to students.

2. **How will we know that they have learned it?** Effective teachers make sure students are clear about what they must learn, and they use assessments to measure student learning and to monitor progress of student learning and their own instructional effectiveness.

3. **What will we do when they haven't learned it?** Effective teachers understand that once they have determined what students must learn and measured whether or not students have learned it, they can then determine what to do when students haven't learned. Effective teachers identify students who need extra help on specific targets previously taught and assessed but not mastered. They reteach the information using different strategies before reassessing students.

4. **What will we do when they already know it?** Effective teachers use assessment information to determine if students have already mastered the content and then extend the learning for proficient students.

Facilitating Classroom Discussion

Effective teachers are masters at facilitating classroom discussions. The teacher has moved from being the *sage on the stage* to being the *guide on the side* (King, 1993). One way effective teachers facilitate discussions is with questioning, sometimes using questions that do not have definitive answers. This strategy encourages students to learn from each other as they listen to one another's perspectives. When there is no definitive answer, students are exposed to one another's thinking and the rationale for what they believe is the answer, therefore gaining new insight. Effective teachers are intentional about the questions they pose, as they typically are higher-order questions that promote critical thinking skills. Author, speaker, and researcher Robert J. Marzano (2013) states, "Questioning is a potentially powerful tool that teachers can use to help students better understand academic content" (p. 76). How an effective teacher keeps the conversation going after posing these questions is just as important. For example, consider the prompt, "That's interesting. Tell me more." Even if it is not the answer the teacher was looking for, a prompt opens the door for further explanation from students (Finley, 2013). Wait time is also an effective strategy (Finley, 2013). Teachers ask a question and wait for students to formulate responses. The longer a teacher waits, the more opportunity students have to answer, especially those students who may take more time to formulate their thoughts than others. In addition to using a variety of questioning techniques directed to the classroom as a whole, teachers can use a variety of questioning strategies to facilitate classroom discussions, including the following.

- **Socratic seminar:** Students are broken into two groups and then sit either in the inner circle or the outer circle. The inner circle is involved in discussing whatever topic is presented, while the outer circle is engaged in a task related to the seminar.

- **Debates:** Students are broken into two groups—one group that is for a particular topic and another group that is against that topic. Each group makes its arguments with rebuttal statements.

- **Speed dating:** Students are paired up and share their thoughts with each other to whatever question the teacher poses. After a minute, students rotate on to the next partner.

- **Agree or disagree:** After a statement is posed to the students, they move to one side of the classroom or another. One side represents agreement and the other side of the classroom represents disagreement. While there, students defend their choice.

- **Conversations:** In groups of four or five, students discuss a question the teacher poses. After a few minutes, two or three students rotate to another group. In the new groups, students discuss another question.

Remember the purpose of facilitating classroom discussion is to engage the students. Teachers should be creating an environment where students are actively learning instead of passively sitting back absorbing information from the teacher.

Using Formative Assessment

Effective teachers use formative assessments (assessments *for* learning) to identify student understanding, clarify what comes next in student learning, trigger and become part of an effective system of intervention for struggling students, and inform and improve their own practices (Stiggins, 2008). *Formative assessments* should diagnose where a student's learning is throughout the learning process. By contrast, *summative assessments* determine what a student knows at the end of the year or unit (Stiggins, 2008).

Teachers should use frequent formative assessments to check for understanding. Otherwise, how do you know if your students are learning what you want them to learn? These frequent checks for understanding allow teachers to adjust their instruction so that all students have learned the material by the time the summative assessment is given. Some examples of formative assessments include the following.

- **Summary cards:** Students write a summary of what they learned in ten to fifteen words, then again in thirty to fifty words, and then again in seventy-five to one hundred words.

- **Whiteboards:** Students use a whiteboard to share their answers, holding it up to show the teacher.

- **Exit slip:** As students leave the classroom, they turn in a 3-2-1 slip with three things they learned, two things they found interesting, and one question they still have.

- **Online platforms:** Using an online platform such as Quizlet (quizlet .com) or Poll Everywhere (polleverywhere.com), post a question that students can respond to immediately using their cell phones.

- **One-minute response:** At the end of the lesson, students have one minute to write about their learning, based on a specific prompt from the teacher.

Now in a PLC, the proper use of assessments, especially if they are teacher team–created common assessments, can have a dramatic effect on student achievement.

Former Superintendent Richard DuFour (2004) argues, "When teacher teams develop common formative assessments throughout the school year, each teacher can identify how his or her students performed on each skill compared with other students" (p. 10). In PLCs, teacher teams work collaboratively to create, administer, and then analyze common assessments to determine students' strengths and areas for improvement. The reason common assessments are so effective is because once they have the common assessment data, teachers work together to determine each student's strengths and areas of needed growth. Then teams determine how to move students toward proficiency. DuFour (2004) notes, "Data will become a catalyst for improved teacher practice only if the teacher has a basis of comparison" (p. 10). In addition, teachers engage in conversations about strategies that work and don't work to refine their future instruction.

Implementing Metacognitive Strategies

Developmental psychologist John H. Flavell (1976) says *metacognition* involves thinking about one's own thinking process, such as one's study skills, memory capabilities, and the ability to monitor learning. *Metacognitive knowledge* is knowledge about one's own cognitive processes and understanding how to regulate those processes to maximize learning. Wikipedia describes metacognition as "cognition about cognition," "thinking about thinking," "knowing about knowing," and becoming "aware of one's awareness" and higher-order thinking ("Metacognition," n.d.). Effective teachers teach metacognition along with content instruction.

Author Stephen M. Fleming (2014) shares five strategies for how effective teachers develop metacognition in their students.

1. **Explicitly teach students about this essential learning skill by defining the term *metacognition*:** Especially with younger students, he recommends a metaphor—such as *driving their brains*—as a concrete way to guide students toward thinking about how they best learn. This metaphor taps into students' desires to master important skills for driving their destiny.

2. **Ask students to describe the benefits and supply examples of driving their brains well:** For example, sometimes we might need to *put on the brakes* (such as by reviewing a reading passage to make sure that we understand it) or *step on the gas* (for instance, by jotting down and

organizing notes for an essay instead of getting stuck on how to start). We need to keep our brains moving in the correct lane and along the best route toward achieving our goals.

3. **Whenever possible, let students choose what they want to read and topics they want to learn more about:** When they are genuinely interested and motivated to learn about a topic of study, students are apt to sustain interest in thinking about a project over the long haul.

4. **Look for opportunities to discuss and apply metacognition across core subjects and in a variety of lessons so students can transfer it for the most benefit:** When a teacher has taught a topic, he or she often asks students to give examples across academics, in interactions with friends and family, and (for older students) on the job. If he or she is teaching younger students, the teacher asks them how their parents might use this strategy in their work.

5. **Model metacognition by talking through problems:** We find that students learn a lot from listening as their teachers use higher-order-thinking strategies aloud. Students often laugh when their teachers make "mistakes," but they learn when their teachers stop, recognize the miscue, and step through the process of correcting. This teachable moment underscores that *everyone* makes mistakes and that mistakes are best seen as opportunities to learn and improve.

Effective teachers use these strategies to help students understand the way they learn. Students annotate texts, understand and use rubrics, and use graphic organizers to organize their thoughts. Effective teachers teach and model these strategies.

Collaborating With Colleagues

The research base in support of collaboration is extensive both inside and outside of education (Carr & Walton, 2014; DuFour et al., 2016; Ronfeldt, Farmer, McQueen, & Grissom, 2015; Ross, 2011; Vescio, Ross, & Adams, 2008) There is compelling evidence that collaboration represents best practice as long as people demonstrate the discipline to collaborate about the right things (DuFour et al., 2016). The question then becomes, What are the *right* things? In PLCs, the right things address the four critical questions of a PLC (DuFour et al., 2016): (1) What do we want students to know and be able to do? (2) How will we know that they have learned it? (3) What will we do when they haven't learned it? and (4) What will we do when they already know it?

Effective teachers move away from talking about problems to working together with colleagues to solve problems. Imagine teachers collaborating by doing the following (Kullar, 2018).

- Providing feedback and sharing ideas with one another
- Reading current research together and discussing how to apply it to their practice
- Conducting action research and then discussing what worked and what didn't work
- Watching one another teach the same lesson and then giving feedback
- Reviewing one another's grading and giving each other feedback
- Analyzing one another's student data and discussing strategies on how to improve

In order for teachers to be able to collaborate with each other, they must have a level of confidence so that they are open to receiving feedback from their peers. In addition to confidence, teachers must communicate well. Teachers need to have the skills to communicate with their colleagues in a respectful manner, even during those emotional moments, and be able to manage and resolve conflicts professionally and effectively. All in all, teachers must understand what it means to be a member of a team—they must always put the needs of the team ahead of their own.

Look Ahead

Now that you have a clearer understanding of what makes a teacher effective, imagine having a school filled with teachers who are passionate and caring, have high expectations, and are reflective. Imagine those teachers always being clear with their purpose, engaging students in discussions, frequently administering formative assessments, engaging in metacognitive strategies, and collaborating with their colleagues. We believe a school filled with effective teachers will absolutely flourish. The most important decisions principals make are to decide who gets to be on the team, who will make a difference in *students'* lives. The outcomes for students who have ineffective teachers are heartbreaking. These students are at high-risk of dropping out, and those who drop out face the following challenges.

- They are three times more likely to be unemployed (Breslow, 2012).

- They are more likely to live in poverty (that is, earn an annual salary of $20,241 or less; Breslow, 2012).

- Females who drop out will live an average of ten and a half years fewer than females who graduate from high school; males who drop out will live an average of thirteen years fewer than males who graduate from high school (Tavernise, 2012).

- They are sixty-three times more likely to be incarcerated (Breslow, 2012).

- The average high school dropout costs taxpayers $292,000 over his or her lifetime (Breslow, 2012).

These staggering and alarming statistics illustrate exactly why it is imperative to hire effective teachers. Many people believe school improvement and student achievement are related to curriculum, class sizes, district funding, and family and community involvement. While these are all important aspects of a great school, the most important influential school-based factor is the teacher (RAND Education, 2012; Stronge & Tucker, 2000). "Compared to any other aspect of schooling, teachers have the greatest impact on student achievement. A well-trained teacher is likely to send more students to college, and can boost a class's lifetime income by $250,000" (Terada, 2019).

In subsequent chapters of this book, we revisit the four characteristics and five processes of effective teachers to offer strategies school leaders can use to build and support new teachers and existing staff.

Next Steps

Use the reproducible "Planning Template to Strengthen the Four Characteristics" (pages 23–24) by brainstorming some strategies you can implement in your school or district to build up and reinforce teachers' passion, caring nature, high expectations, and capacity for reflection.

Use the reproducible "Assessment of Teaching Practices" (page 25) to evaluate the teachers in your school or district. This will give you information on where your teachers are as a staff in each of the five practices outlined in this chapter. By knowing which practices are the strongest in your building, you can determine not only what professional development you need but also what kinds of teachers you need to hire to fill gaps on your staff.

REFLECTION QUESTIONS

1. Consider the four effective teacher characteristics: (1) passion, (2) a caring nature, (3) high expectations, and (4) capacity for reflection. Which one of these characteristics is the hardest to find in a teacher? The hardest to instill? The hardest to maintain? Why?

2. Why is it so important to incorporate a collaborative culture in your school to help build effective teachers?

3. Consider the five effective teacher processes: (1) achieving clarity, (2) facilitating classroom discussion, (3) using formative assessment, (4) implementing metacognitive strategies, and (5) collaborating with colleagues. As a school or district leader, which one of these processes is currently your strongest? In other words, you know teachers engage in this process well. Which process is a challenge? How can you overcome that challenge?

4. If your school is a PLC or in the process of transformation, consider how you can ensure all teachers are focused on the four critical questions of a PLC: (1) What do we want students to know and be able to do? (2) How will we know that they have learned it? (3) What will we do when they haven't learned it? and (4) What will we do when they already know it?

Planning Template to Strengthen the Four Characteristics

Use the following template to examine the four characteristics and brainstorm strategies you plan to use in your school.

Characteristics	Example Strategies
Passion	• End a meeting with an inspirational message or song. • Remind teachers why they chose the profession. Have them write their *why* on a small card. Frame it, and give it to teachers as a constant reminder of their why. • Have teachers think about a teacher who made a difference in their lives and discuss how they can be that teacher for someone else. • As a staff, create a *passion plan* that outlines what steps or actions they can take. • Create a professional learning calendar with a variety of topics and events that teachers can pick from.
Your Plan:	
A Caring Nature	• Involve teachers in conversations about specific students to learn more about their home life. • Take teachers on a road trip on the school bus so they can see the neighborhoods their students come from. • Create a mentoring program at your school where every teacher has to adopt one student who they mentor and advocate for. • Create a *silent shepherd* program at your school where staff identify students who need extra attention. Then assign a staff member to pay special attention to each student. • Survey your students so teachers can see how their students perceive them.
Your Plan:	

page 1 of 2

High Expectations	• Ensure that a PLC exists in your school to ensure expectations for students are high and that all teachers on the team are doing everything they can to guarantee students meet those expectations. • Monitor every team's common assessments to see those high expectations. • Don't allow teachers to let students take a zero on an assignment. Teachers who have high expectations will make sure that students not only do the work assigned but also do it at the expected level. Instead, students should work during an intervention block of time (or study hall or some other structured time) to make sure students complete their work.
Your Plan:	
Capacity for Reflection	• Give teachers experiences and opportunities to reflect on their practices by involving them in various activities as well as reflection exercises. • Facilitate peer observations. • Have teachers videotape themselves teaching. • Ask teachers to shadow a student. • Help teachers reflect by answering structured questions.
Your Plan:	

Building Your Building © 2020 Solution Tree Press • SolutionTree.com
Visit **go.SolutionTree.com/leadership** to download this free reproducible.

Assessment of Teaching Practices

Assess your teachers on their use of the teaching practices included in the following chart.

	1	2	3	4
Achieving Clarity	Less than half of our teachers (below 50 percent) can deconstruct standards and identify learning targets.	Just over half of our teachers (50 to 69 percent) can deconstruct standards and identify learning targets.	Most of our teachers (70 to 90 percent) can deconstruct standards and identify learning targets.	Almost all our teachers (91 to 100 percent) can deconstruct standards and identify learning targets.
Facilitating Classroom Discussion	Less than half of our teachers (below 50 percent) use engaging strategies to facilitate classroom discussion.	Just over half of our teachers (50 to 69 percent) use engaging strategies to facilitate classroom discussion.	Most of our teachers (70 to 90 percent) use engaging strategies to facilitate classroom discussion.	Almost all our teachers (91 to 100 percent) use engaging strategies to facilitate classroom discussion.
Using Formative Assessments	Less than half of our teachers (below 50 percent) use frequent formative assessments.	Just over half of our teachers (50 to 69 percent) use frequent formative assessments.	Most of our teachers (70 to 90 percent) use frequent formative assessments.	Almost all our teachers (91 to 100 percent) use frequent formative assessments.
Implementing Metacognitive Strategies	Less than half of our teachers (below 50 percent) use metacognitive strategies with students.	Just over half of our teachers (50 to 69 percent) use metacognitive strategies with students.	Most of our teachers (70 to 90 percent) use metacognitive strategies with students.	Almost all our teachers (91 to 100 percent) use metacognitive strategies with students.
Collaborating With Colleagues	Less than half of our teachers (below 50 percent) collaborate with their peers.	Just over half of our teachers (50 to 69 percent) collaborate with their peers.	Most of our teachers (70 to 90 percent) collaborate with their peers.	Almost all our teachers (91 to 100 percent) collaborate with their peers.

CHAPTER 2

Hiring Practices

*The secret of my success is that we have gone to exceptional
lengths to hire the best people in the world.*
—Steve Jobs

> *Principal Margaret James has had a challenging year. She has been principal
> of Lincoln Middle School for five years, and in that time, she has experienced
> significant teacher turnover. This year was especially difficult because of a new
> district initiative, which, although challenging to adjust to, will no doubt lead
> to higher levels of learning for all students. Consequently, Principal James has
> more teacher vacancies to fill for the next school year than usual. Some may
> look at this as a problem; however, Principal James considers it an opportunity
> to hire some fresh staff members to make sure that her school is focused on the
> district's new initiatives. She decides to examine her past hiring practices to
> think about how to ensure she hires the best person for each new opening.*

This chapter focuses on processes and tools school leaders like Principal James can use to hire great teachers to build their building. In this chapter, we cover ongoing initiatives schools should implement year-round—not just when there are vacancies. We then shift to the hiring process (covering reviewing applications and résumés), the interview process, and alternatives to traditional interview techniques. We provide opportunities for you to reflect on your practice and include many reproducible tools to help you during the hiring process.

Before we begin by exploring ongoing initiatives, we want to strongly recommend that school leaders involve their teachers in the recruiting and hiring process. "Bringing teachers fully into the hiring process not only helps find the best teachers for the job, but it also helps grow teacher leadership" (Clement, 2013, p. 71). In addition, teachers involved in the hiring process will likely feel compelled to help their selected candidate be successful in his or her new position. The best teachers to bring into the hiring process are the teachers who will ultimately work with the new hire. This could be members of the department team, interdisciplinary team, or even a vertical team. The critical element is that the other team of teachers has buy-in and feels valued. The level of mentoring and support teachers provide will be more impactful since they have a stake in ensuring the new teacher's success.

Ongoing Initiatives

Many school leaders make the mistake of waiting to focus on hiring activities until there is a vacancy—until they need to hire. This is a mistake. There are ongoing initiatives school leaders can implement to put their school in the best position to hire great teachers when the time comes. In this section, we discuss marketing the positives, creating a welcoming environment, encouraging upward mobility, creating college partnerships, defining your needs, and recruiting year-round.

Market the Positives

Heidi Cohen (2011) states that marketing is the means by which an organization communicates to, connects with, and engages its target audience to convey the value of and ultimately sell its products and services. Schools or districts that are high achieving and become destination districts for families and educators market by showcasing their great results.

School leaders and staff are in the best position to market their school. Those working in the school have a front-row seat to all the incredible things going on. Too often, these positives are overlooked, and news becomes the inevitable negative event. So, school leaders should always publicize the great things happening in their school. One benefit of such marketing efforts is that a positive image will set the tone for how the community perceives the school, and this community includes potential future teachers. When there is a job opening, the school's positive reputation will draw a pool of high-quality applicants because great teachers will want to work there.

A key to successful marketing is to know who you are as a school. This is where being a PLC is particularly helpful because members of PLCs have worked collaboratively to determine their school's mission, vision, values, and goals. They know what their school stands for; what they as a school want to become; the commitments they have made to one another and students to make the school's vision a reality; and those things they hope to achieve as a school. These are important foundational elements to express in your marketing so your school can attract teachers who want to be a part of a school with a clear vision and strategy.

So, what should school leaders focus on to get the word out in the community about the great things happening in their school? William D. Parker (2017) explains seven ways to maximize messaging.

1. Commit to a daily and weekly broadcast of amazing moments. Encourage teachers and students to adopt that mindset as well.

2. Practice and schedule messaging so that you build momentum around those messages.

3. Be present and mindful when you are with students. Instead of just doing walkthroughs or observations by using a tech tool, force yourself to look into the faces of students and teachers and identify what kind of learning is happening.

4. Include teachers and students in communicating what learning is taking place in school. Whether that is bringing a team of teachers to board members or students demonstrating what they're learning, let people hear from the products of our educational environments—students themselves.

5. Give teachers permission to share their best ideas. If you have a techy-teacher, include him or her to share with other teachers.

6. Commit to a weekly newsletter that can be sent to parents and community members so they have an image-rich summary of awesome happenings. Give parents a positive context for your schools so that problems or conflicts are always in the context of positive conversations you've already initiated.

7. Don't be afraid to oversaturate your audience, parents or community with positive moments.

The most obvious place to start is your school's presence on the internet and social media. Your school website is a place for potential hires to visit to gain an understanding of your mission, vision, collective commitments, and goals, which are the foundation of the PLC process. Your mission will convey your purpose. For example, at Olentangy Orange Middle School in Lewis Center, Ohio, its mission is to facilitate maximum learning for all—students, staff, parents, and the community. Their vision is to become a national model of excellence. Their collective commitments answer the following statements.

- What promises are you willing to make to your colleagues that will support our success in achieving our mission and vision?

- When your students leave you, how do you want them to be different, as people, as a result of being with you all yearlong?

- What are your fundamental, bedrock beliefs about your role in making sure that all students learn at high levels?

Potential hires will also look for a message from the principal to see if their beliefs align with those of the school leader.

Twitter and Facebook have emerged as powerful tools for schools. These tools are a great way to showcase what is occurring in real time, such as class discussions, concerts, sporting events, and other examples of students and teachers in action. Anything that is positive in the school can and should be shared.

Always have pamphlets and brochures on hand that summarize your school's successes, and make these materials available outside the school office. These tools are a valuable way to build a positive reputation in your community and let prospective teachers know about your school. At the end of this chapter on page 44, we provide the reproducible "School Marketing Template" to help you collect information to include in your printed marketing efforts.

Also, although it might sound simplistic, utilize your teachers and perhaps even parents to help market your school. Encourage them to tell their friends and neighbors about your school.

Create a Welcoming Environment

Be sure to create a welcoming environment in your building. The front office has a critical role as the face and voice of the school. Office staff are usually the first people visitors from outside the school come in contact with. We always say, "When you answer the phone, make sure the person on the other end hears a smile." A neat, organized, and friendly front office sends a positive message not only to students and families but also to potential job candidates that your school would be a great place to work.

Schools that function as PLCs make their mission, vision, values, and goals clear to all who visit by posting these foundational elements in the office, hallways, and classrooms. Many schools will have samples of student work throughout the halls and entrance. We have also seen schools in which flags of the countries from which their students come hang in the halls. Anything that leaders can do to make everyone feel welcome is important.

Encourage Upward Mobility

Another way to attract teachers to your district is to provide opportunities for professional growth and internal promotion. By promoting teachers internally in the district, you establish good public relations for the district. Promoting from within inspires other teachers (Douglas, 2012) as well as provides another reason for candidates to be interested in your district—the benefit of internal promotion. When teachers are promoted from within, they feel that the district is committed to them. Part of our job as leaders is to foster and grow the talents of teachers and help them gain positions that best utilize their talents. We are not arguing that leaders should always promote from within; rather, we advocate a balanced approach of both practices (external hiring and internal promotion). Leaders should be aware, however, that if they always give the promotions to external candidates, they may not recruit talented new teachers who have aspirations of doing more in their careers. Either way, always ensure your district is open to new changes and ideas whether you promote from within or bring in people from outside your school.

Create College Partnerships

Orange Middle School in Lewis Center, Ohio, has always opened its doors to student teachers from universities, including The Ohio State University; however, in 2014, the school embarked on a very different approach to partnering with colleges and universities. In addition to taking a few student teachers from several universities each year, the school also trained all of the education students from one school—Otterbein University in Westerville, Ohio—in the PLC process through-out their entire college careers.

It started with several Otterbein students who were doing their preservice train-ing at Orange Middle School and then reporting what they had learned about this PLC to their professors. The professors liked what they were hearing and asked if all their preservice and student teachers could go through Orange Middle School. In addition, the professors asked if they could teach their methods classes at the middle school so students would have easy access to Orange teachers.

Orange Middle School is creating a pipeline of prospective new teachers capa-ble of coming into their school and district. Since 2014, Orange Middle School has hired six teachers who went through this process at Otterbein. The school handpicks the best of the best—from more than 150 applicants for one job—who embrace the PLC philosophy.

Define Your Needs

Before hiring, we recommend knowing exactly what your hiring needs are. Your hiring needs must be more specific than just *a science teacher* or *a fourth-grade teacher*. What specific qualities are you looking for to complete your team? What unique skills are you looking for to strengthen your school? The reproduc-ible "Hiring Needs Checklist" (page 45) at the end of this chapter will help you think through your specific hiring needs. Meet with members of the teacher team with a vacancy to discuss needed skills and strengths to get a clearer picture of the characteristics potential job candidates should have.

Recruit Year-Round

Schools and districts should recruit and screen potential candidates all year long—not only when there is a vacancy. Being prepared early, instead of waiting until later when the strongest candidates are taken, helps make hiring early possible. The Cobb County School District in Marietta, Georgia, created a robust recruiting plan that allows the district to begin recruiting proactively. Its recruiting efforts begin with a dedicated full-time recruiting supervisor, who is in charge of recruiting effective teachers and staff. The district has several administrators who go through a stan-dardized training in recruiting and interviewing each year, and then go to various recruiting events across the region with the recruiting supervisor. Together, this recruiting team attends about forty recruiting events each year, typically in about ten states. This team interviews approximately one thousand candidates each year.

At these recruiting events, the district uses iPads to administer the district's proprietary Quick Pick Evaluation System (QPES). This is a system the district created to help with its recruitment efforts. First, information about the candidate is entered into the system. And then after entering the candidate's answers into the database, this system's five-question screening tool rates the candidate's answers. Principals can see the collected and rated information when they access individuals' application files. This system allows the district the opportunity to gather information about applicants to reduce the time principals spend reviewing applications. Principals can search and sort applicants based on QPES scores.

In addition, Cobb County School District displays what it calls a *wall of grandeur* at recruiting events. This wall of advertising for the district is bright and attention grabbing. This approach differs from that of other districts, which typically use only a table with a school logo on the tablecloth for their marketing materials. The wall makes the district stand out and attracts applicants.

Finally, Cobb County School District hosts two large, heavily advertised job fairs in the spring and requires principals to attend. One is for elementary schools and the other is for middle and high schools. In total, approximately 2,500 candidates from all over the United States attend. Principals usually hire difficult-to-fill positions in specific fields of teaching on the spot, as well as applicants who really stand out.

Cobb County School District has made it a priority to "Make Cobb the best place to teach, lead, and learn." This commitment is evident in Cobb's recruiting and retention practices. In 2019, the district received the honor of being on Forbes best employers list (Valet, 2019)—a list that rarely includes school districts.

The Hiring Process

In this section, we examine the process of reviewing applications and résumés and then shift to the interview process itself by looking at critical questions the school leader and interview panel of teachers must ask. We follow with alternative interview practices to consider and recommendations for reference checking.

Reviewing Applications and Résumés

Together with the collaborative teacher team with the vacancy, leaders should review the applications and résumés. First, ensure the applicants are qualified for the job and meet all the basic requirements. It is important for someone to do initial reviews and interviews to weed out applicants who don't meet minimum requirements. Then review qualified candidates' applications to see evidence of the characteristics of an effective teacher. Use a checklist to determine which applicants the team believes it should invite for an interview. See the reproducible "Résumé and Application Checklist" at the end of the chapter on page 46 for guidance.

Interviewing

As authors Autumn Tooms and Alicia Crowe (2004) note in their article *Hiring Good Teachers: The Interview Process*, "A professionally conducted interview builds a cultural dynamic that may eventually result in larger and stronger candidate pools because you have set the tone for a school environment in which people want to work" (p. 53). Leaders should take time to establish what their school's interview process will look like. Following are some topics to consider.

How Many Tiers?

How many levels (or tiers) of interviews will the candidate go through? For example, if you have three tiers in your interview process, it may begin with the teacher team with the job opening conducting the first screening interview. Candidates who succeed at that tier then move on to the next interview. The team will use this interview to determine two or three candidates to move to the final tier. Another team could conduct this second interview. The top two to three candidates from the second tier then move on to the final tier. This multitiered approach allows you to eliminate candidates and have multiple conversations with the candidate you eventually select.

Also determine what you will include in each tier (interview). For example, will each candidate receive a tour after the first interview, or will the tour be reserved for only the top two or three candidates after the second interview? Tours help engage candidates in informal conversation and also allow you to show your school and the culture and tone of the building.

In addition, decide what you want candidates to bring to the interview. For example, do you want them to bring sample lesson plans or unit plans? Should they bring some kind of a portfolio? Be specific about what each interview (tier) will include, and notify candidates ahead of the interview so they can prepare their materials.

Who Will Attend?

When hiring, it is important to select a candidate who is the right match for the school and the specific team. "Investing time in bringing teachers into the hiring process and training them well . . . gives schools the best chance to make good matches" (Clement, 2013, p. 71). The principal, assistant principal, or a teacher should never be the only one to conduct an interview. The interview process should include multiple people with different perspectives from beginning to end, and these individuals should be trained in the hiring process. For instance, you can bring a counselor or a teacher leader into an interview, or a staff person from a different department who can contribute a unique perspective to the interview process. These staff members bring perspectives outside of the content area. You could also bring in one or two people who will be working with the candidate directly, if not the entire team. In other words, one person should not conduct the entire interview process; bringing teachers and other staff members in will provide a broader perspective.

It's important to reiterate that, ultimately, it is the principal's decision. A principal should never let a team make the final decision; however, the principal should listen to and consider the opinions and feedback of involved teams. If a principal and team are not on the same page about a candidate, they should have candid conversations about the reasons behind their differences in opinion in order to facilitate understanding and lead the principal to the best decision.

Who Will Ask Questions?

Once you decide who will be on the interview panel, the next step is to prepare the questions in advance, together as a team, and then decide who will ask which questions. During pretraining with the interview panel, discuss what you as a team are looking for in the candidates' answers and how the panel will rate the answers. Teachers on the panel should ask questions related to the curriculum—who else knows the curriculum better?—in addition to questions that will help members decide if the potential candidate will be a good fit on the collaborative team. See the reproducible "Sample Interview Questions" (pages 47–48) at the end of this chapter for potential interview questions to ask teacher candidates.

The principal can ask the candidates questions related to the school's mission, such as, "Will you help advance the school's mission?" At some point during the interview, talk about your school. As Tooms and Crowe (2004) state, "Nothing helps people understand more about a school community than the principal bragging a little. How you convey your love of your school may very well end up being the deciding factor for a stellar candidate" (p. 53).

How Will We Arrange the Room?

Prepare the room or office where the interview will take place. How do you want the chairs arranged, and where should the candidate be seated? The candidate can sit at the head of the table while the interview panel members sit around him or her; or everyone can sit in a circle, including the candidate; or the candidate can be standing in front of the panel members sitting in rows, and so on. There are many possibilities. We prefer an interview in which everyone is in close proximity, usually around a table. What is more important than the arrangement is making the interview setting inviting and welcoming. Interviewing is stressful; the more comfortable the environment, the more relaxed the conversation, which helps school leaders and team members truly get to know an applicant in a short period of time. Also plan to offer water and provide any materials you want the candidate to have during the interview.

What Questions Will We Ask?

There are two main types of questions to ask in an interview: (1) situational and (2) behavioral. *Situational questions* ask candidates about the future—how they would resolve an issue. *Behavioral questions* ask candidates about their past—how they resolved an issue.

With situational questions, the panel gives the candidate a situation to gauge how he or she would handle it. For example, "A parent calls you and tells you he is really upset because his son is failing your class and it's all your fault. What is your response to the parent?" There are many benefits of asking situational questions. You get a glimpse of how the candidate will handle common situations. You get an understanding of the candidate's thought process and how he or she prioritizes and uses problem-solving skills. You learn about what the candidate values. You get a clearer picture of a candidate's strengths. Using the traditional interview question, "What are your strengths?" often results in a surface-level description detached from real-life application. Situational questions ask the candidate to apply his or her strengths and articulate the response based on his or her knowledge and skill sets. Think about how that could help assess the candidate's ability to think strategically.

Behavioral questions ask the candidate about how he or she handled a past situation. For example, "Tell us about a time when you had a conflict with a colleague." The benefit of behavioral questions is that they allow the candidate to reflect on actual experiences. How the candidate behaved or solved a problem in the past will be an indicator on how he or she will behave and problem solve in the future. In addition, behavioral questions give the panel insight into the candidate's previous experience. For example, if you ask a question about how the candidate handled a difficult student and the candidate struggles to answer that question, this could indicate he or she has limited experience in that area, which may not be what you and the team are looking for in a candidate.

Because both types of questions have benefits, we recommend creating a balance of behavioral and situational interview questions to gain the best information possible about whether or not the candidate is the perfect fit for your school.

In PLCs, it is essential to also ask questions regarding the candidate's fit. DuFour et al. (2016) state that asking questions such as "Will you support our PLC process?" is ineffective because of course the candidate is going to say *yes*. Instead, ask questions that really give insight into what the candidate believes about the PLC process. Ask situational questions that could give you perspective on the candidate's thinking about the three big ideas. DuFour et al. (2016) provide some interview questions for candidates that reflect the processes in a PLC:

- If you were assigned to a teaching team and encouraged to collaborate, on what questions or issues do you believe the team should focus its efforts? (p. 192)

- It's the end of your first year. I ask you to provide me with evidence you have been an effective teacher. What will you give me? (p. 192)

- One of your colleagues states that there is little a teacher can do to help a student who is just not interested in learning. Would you respond, and if so, how would you respond? (p. 191)

- In what ways, if any, is the PLC process different from traditional schooling? (p. 192)

We provide a reproducible bank of sample interview questions to use for a variety of positions at the end of this chapter (see the "Interview Question Bank," pages 49–55). In addition, we provide a reproducible recording form to use during interviews to take notes as candidates respond to questions (see the "Interview Recording Form," pages 56–57).

What Is the Role of the Interviewer?

Don't assume members of your panel will know how to act during the interview. Go over the key professional behaviors you expect from interviewers (see the "Interview Panel Commitment Form," page 58). Begin with appearance; all interviewers should dress professionally for interviews. This portrays an expectation of professionalism at your school. We also recommend instructing panel members not to talk too much. Remember, the interview is for a candidate to convince you and the panel that he or she is the right fit for your school. He or she can't do that if one panel member is doing all the talking.

Everyone must prepare for the interview. Has everyone reviewed the applications and résumés? Does everyone know what questions the panel will ask? Panel members should be aware of their nonverbal behaviors to ensure they reflect professionalism. Remember, candidates are most likely nervous, so they will be looking at your nonverbal language to get cues on whether you think they are doing a good job or not. Keep smiling and nodding to give all your interviewees reassurance and to create a safe environment during the interview. Pay attention during the entire interview. Remember, the candidate is doing his or her best and deserves the panel's undivided attention. Put your devices away and be completely present during the interviews. In addition, never ask illegal questions. Work with your district staff to learn what those illegal questions are and stay away from them. According to the U.S. Equal Employment Opportunity Commission (n.d.), illegal job interview questions are those that solicit information from job candidates that could be used to discriminate against them. Asking questions about a candidate's race, religion, or gender could open a school up to a discrimination lawsuit.

Lastly, after the interview is over, take the time to walk out the candidate. As you walk with him or her, let the candidate know you will be in touch and your time line for the decision. We recommend a time line of two weeks from start to finish.

Determine what your follow-up activities will be. Will you send an email to the candidate or mail him or her a thank-you card? What will you do for the candidates who do not get a job offer? Will you call them or send them some kind of notification? Will you encourage them to apply again, or will you keep them in mind for future positions? Your follow-up process says a lot about your school and is a critical piece in the marketing of future positions.

How Do We Evaluate Truthfulness?

Sometimes, despite our best efforts, we do not identify the best candidate for the position. Unfortunately, sometimes this is the result of a candidate telling the panel members what he or she thinks they want to hear—and not being truthful about his or her experience or goals. It's not uncommon for candidates to stretch or embellish the truth—after all, they want the job! It is the responsibility of the panel to do what it can to ensure the candidate is providing accurate answers during the interview. Following are some tips that may help.

- **Check for consistency:** Ask different questions with the same focus to see if you get the same answers. In other words, ask similar questions to check for consistency. For example, ask, "Why do you want to teach at this school?" and then follow up after a few more questions with a similar question such as, "What about this school are you most excited about?"

- **Evaluate body language:** Look at a candidate's body language. Notice if candidates are fidgeting a lot or moving their legs around or tapping their feet. This could be a sign of nervousness, of course, but it is also a sign that a candidate might not be truthful. Also observe how the candidate sits down—is his or her arms crossed across the body or does he or she appear relaxed. "Because people are not always aware they are communicating nonverbally, body language is often more honest than an individual's verbal pronouncements, which are consciously crafted to accomplish the speaker's objectives" (Navarro, 2008, p. 4).

- **Look for eye contact:** We have long believed that if people don't look you in the eye, they are lying. However, this could also be a cultural behavior since, in some cultures, looking at others in the eye while talking is considered disrespectful. Despite this possibility, it is something to look for.

- **Be aware of voice changes:** A sudden change in the candidate's voice could be a sign of deception (for example, if, all of a sudden, the candidate's pitch goes up or down while answering a question). Look for other changes in voice, such as long pauses, the candidate not being able to get his or her words out, stammering, or throat clearing as further evidence of deception (Navarro, 2008).

Educational consultant Tim Brown (2016) has aptly commented, "I just want every teacher to be the teacher they said they were going to be during the interview." Take a few moments to think about what your current teachers said during their interviews. Are they truly who they said they were? Are they treating students the way they said they were going to treat them? Are they calling parents with praise (not just with criticism)? Are they collaborating with their colleagues and differentiating instruction? It's always a risk and a leap of faith to accept what a candidate says during an interview as the absolute truth. In order to maximize the probability that you are hiring the best teacher for the job, consider some different ways of interviewing candidates so the panel gets a complete picture.

Interviewing Alternatives

Sometimes, no matter how hard you try to make the interview process effective in finding the best candidates, you do not necessarily accomplish that goal. As a result, we would like to offer some alternative practices to the traditional interview—teach a lesson, meet and greets, speed interviews, recruiting socials, and tests—that might help you pick the best candidate possible for your school.

Teach a Lesson

In our experience, having candidates teach a lesson is highly effective. When we use this strategy, the "class" is the interview team of teachers, administrators, counselors, and usually one office staff member. We give very general instructions, such as, "Teach a lesson on a topic relevant to the grade level. You will have forty-five minutes to teach." This is a great way to see how a candidate will react to a very stressful situation. Most people interviewing for a teaching position have experience teaching children; but when the teaching happens in front of adults, the dynamics can change, making the situation more stressful. Another option is to allow the candidate to teach a real class while you and the other interviewers observe the lesson. This task may be difficult for many candidates since they haven't built relationships with the students; however, it provides invaluable information for the interview panel members who must make sure they are hiring the best person for the job.

Meet and Greets

Host a meet and greet at a local coffee shop or similar location so the panel members can get to know the candidate to see if he or she will fit into your school's culture. This is a great way to eliminate candidates if you're in the beginning stages of the interview process, or a great way to decide between your top two candidates if you're in the final stage of the process. Either way, it is a great additional step in the interview process.

Speed Interviews

Speed interviews call for a school to bring in all candidates at the same time. Set up the room like a speed-dating event, where one row of chairs is for the interviewers and the other row across is for the candidates. Each round of interviews should last for a set amount of time. After the time is up, the candidates move one chair over and someone else interviews him or her. By the end of all the rounds, the interviewers should have interviewed everyone individually and have insight about which candidates they felt were the best for the school. Arrange for a debriefing time when the interviewers can compare notes and discuss who they feel would be the best fit—or perhaps which candidates should now come back for a formal interview to achieve a balanced interviewing approach with traditional and nontraditional practices.

Recruiting Socials

Invite all possible candidates to a social event at your school, maybe for coffee or lunch (depending on your budget). During this social event, get to know the candidates and see if your teachers gravitate toward some candidates more than others. Schools can use this strategy in addition to formal interviews; you and the panel can invite back candidates who seem to be a good fit for the formal interview.

Tests

Providing candidates with some kind of a test can also give another layer of information to help you and the panel decide on the best candidate for your school. A test could be having the candidate watch a video of a teacher teaching a lesson, with the panel asking questions about how the candidate would improve the lesson. Or, give the candidate several problems (for example, a student with grades that show he or she is struggling, a parent who continues to send angry emails, and so on), and have the candidate write a plan of action to help resolve the problems.

Checking References

No matter what method you use to select the best candidate, never skip the reference-check process. As a principal or school leader, probably the most important thing you do when it comes to hiring effectively is to take the time to conduct reference checks (see the reproducible "Sample Questions for Reference Checks" [page 59] at the end of the chapter for sample questions to ask a reference). A candidate may blow you away in an interview—until you contact a reference who tells you something completely different. The best way to predict the candidate's work performance is to find out about his or her past work performance. Paul Slezak (2015), cofounder and CEO of RecruitLoop (https://recruitloop.com), identifies the following tips for effective reference checks.

- Conduct two verbal reference checks.
- Plan your questions ahead of time.
- Check the credibility of the references.

We also advocate talking to people who are somehow connected to the candidate's references. The reality is that no candidate is going to use a reference who is going to say bad things about him or her. That is why if the candidate has included the assistant principal as a reference, you should call the principal to get his or her thoughts.

It's also a good idea to find out as much as you can about the candidate's digital footprint. If you don't, students and parents will do it for you! We always check to see what potential candidates have posted on their Facebook, LinkedIn, Twitter, and Instagram accounts. It is important to keep up with social media to see what people are posting. You can learn a lot about candidates just based on the information they post on their social media accounts. By taking a look at a potential teacher's digital footprint, we can be better informed if he or she will be a good fit.

Look Ahead

It is crucial to hire the best candidates possible. School leaders have many strategies at their disposal to do so, beginning with a focus on ongoing initiatives to build a school's positive reputation, encouraging a culture of upward mobility, creating partnerships, and recruiting year-round. By implementing the hiring practices for interviewing we describe in this chapter, principals and district leaders can ensure they chose the best candidates available to them. This process will also open the door to matching up new teachers with a mentor, someone to guide and coach them throughout their first year.

Next Steps

Use the "School Marketing Template" (page 44) to summarize all the great things happening at your school—kind of like a bragging sheet.

Complete the "Hiring Needs Checklist" (page 45) *before* actually looking for candidates. This tool will help you and your team have a clearer idea of what specific skills you are looking for in a candidate.

Use the "Résumé and Application Checklist" (page 46) when reviewing applications and résumés. This tool can help to determine which applicants to invite to an interview.

Use the "Sample Interview Questions" (pages 47–48) to identify candidates' strengths and weaknesses as they relate to the four teacher characteristics and five effective teaching processes we described in chapter 1 (page 9).

Refer to the "Interview Question Bank" (pages 49–55) to select questions for a variety of different positions to use in interviews with candidates.

The "Interview Recording Form" (pages 56–57) is useful for taking notes during each candidate's interview.

The "Interview Panel Commitment Form" (page 58) helps the panel members understand the expectations and commit to their roles as interviewers. The commitment form also has a scoring rubric so the panel can sign off to indicate they are aware and understand how to score each of the candidate's answers (in addition to the other stipulations).

"Sample Questions for Reference Checks" (page 59) are sample questions school leaders can ask the applicants' references. Be sure to check with your local laws and board policies on which questions are legal or illegal to ask.

REFLECTION QUESTIONS

1. What are some products you can create to help market your school all yearlong?

2. How can you establish partnerships with local colleges?

3. What are some ways you can strengthen your interview process now? After reading this chapter, what changes will you make to your interview process?

4. When looking at the candidate's digital footprint, what are some things you should look for?

REPRODUCIBLE

School Marketing Template

School Name:

School Mission:

School Vision:

School Values (Collective Commitments):

School Goals:

    1.

    2.

    3.

Initiatives:

    1.

    2.

    3.

Celebrations:

Hiring Needs Checklist

Our Hiring Needs

These are the skills or qualifications we are looking for in this particular vacancy.

	Yes—We Need This Skill for This Vacancy (No one on the team has this skill.)	No—We Don't Need This Skill for This Vacancy (Someone else on the team already has this skill.)
Specific Certification		
Bilingual		
Technology Skills		
Experience with PLCs		
Data Expertise		
Leadership Experience		
Teaching Experience		
Response to Intervention (RTI) Knowledge		
Assessment Knowledge		
Differentiation Knowledge		
Other:		
Other:		
Other:		
Other:		
Other:		

Building Your Building © 2020 Solution Tree Press • SolutionTree.com
Visit **go.SolutionTree.com/leadership** to download this free reproducible.

REPRODUCIBLE

Résumé and Application Checklist

Candidate Name	Teaching Experience	Highest Education	Certifications	Accomplishments	Special Skills	Appearance and Writing Quality of Résumé 1–5 (5 is excellent)
Example: Mr. Doe	Five years	Master's	Social Studies (K–6)	Increased pass rate on state test by 5 percent	Technology Student Council sponsor Bilingual	4

Building Your Building © 2020 Solution Tree Press • SolutionTree.com
Visit **go.SolutionTree.com/leadership** to download this free reproducible.

Sample Interview Questions

Interview Questions for Effective Teacher Characteristics and Processes

Eighteen Questions to Assess Effective Teacher Characteristics

Passion

1. What do you do outside the classroom to help motivate and inspire students?

2. Describe a situation where you were so passionately focused on something that you lost track of time.

3. In your field of education, what is one big problem you would like to solve? Why?

4. Sell yourself. Why do we need you on our team?

A Caring Nature

5. What frustrates you about students? Why?

6. How do you show your students you care about them?

7. Describe a time when you went above and beyond for a student.

8. Why do you like working with students?

High Expectations

9. One of your students does not turn in a major assignment on the due date. What would you do?

10. Describe your classroom management philosophy and plan.

11. What's your superpower? How will you ensure your students find their superpower?

12. What do you want for your students in five years?

Capacity for Reflection

13. How do you stay current with education trends, research, and practices?

14. Describe a time when you self-reflected and changed something as a result.

Building Your Building © 2020 Solution Tree Press • SolutionTree.com
Visit **go.SolutionTree.com/leadership** to download this free reproducible.

15. What have you done professionally that, after self-reflection, is an experience you will never repeat?

16. Describe a mistake you made. What was it and how did you learn from it?

17. What book are you currently reading to help you be a better teacher? What have you learned from it?

18. What is the last professional development opportunity you participated in? What did you learn from it?

Ten Questions to Assess Effective Teacher Processes

Achieving Clarity

1. How will you advance our school's mission statement?

2. Sometimes people may distract you from the work by complaining about students or other things. How do you remain focused on the right work?

Facilitating Classroom Discussion

3. What would a great classroom discussion look like?

4. If you were teaching a lesson on this standard _____, what two higher-order questions would you ask students?

Using Formative Assessment

5. Give three examples of formative assessments you use in your classroom.

6. What do you do with formative assessment data?

Implementing Metacognitive Strategies

7. Give an example of how you used a graphic organizer in one of your lessons.

8. What makes a rubric effective?

Collaborating With Colleagues

9. Share a time when you had difficulty working with a colleague. How did you handle it?

10. After sharing your data in your collaborative team meeting with your colleagues, you realize that you had the highest number of students fail the common formative assessment. What would you do?

Building Your Building © 2020 Solution Tree Press • SolutionTree.com
Visit **go.SolutionTree.com/leadership** to download this free reproducible.

Interview Question Bank

Teacher Questions

Source: Adapted from Hodges, 2012.

Achievement Drive

1. What are your teaching goals?

2. How do you measure your success as a teacher?

3. What motivates you to achieve goals or be successful?

4. How do you keep yourself motivated when you have challenging days in the classroom?

5. In your past work experience, what have you done that you consider truly creative?

6. What is the last book you read? What did you learn from it?

7. Describe a time you were given feedback. What was the feedback and how did you respond?

Student and Parent Relationships

8. What are the most important things a teacher must accomplish during the first few days of school?

9. What do you think will provide you the greatest satisfaction in teaching?

10. If you could require one characteristic, quality, or attribute of all teachers, what would it be?

11. How important are student and parent relationships to teaching?

12. How do you create student and parent relationships?

Classroom Structure and Planning

13. What teaching approaches, techniques, or methods are most effective for you?

14. How can you get students excited about learning?

15. What do you do when students don't do well on a test?

16. What do you do when a lesson or strategy doesn't appear to be working?

Building Your Building © 2020 Solution Tree Press • SolutionTree.com
Visit **go.SolutionTree.com/leadership** to download this free reproducible.

17. How will you specifically differentiate instruction for all students?

18. Give us an overview and needs assessment (academic, athletic, public perception, and so on) of our school.

Staff Relationships

19. How important is it for coworkers to be your friends?

20. What kind of support do you need from your principal?

21. What are your expectations of your principal?

22. Explain what collaboration looks like to you.

Digging Deeper

23. What is your specialty as a teacher?

24. What do you do really well?

25. What type of students do you like to work with?

26. Tell me what type of students you believe you can teach most effectively?

27. If you were to teach here, what could you bring to our school to really make a difference?

28. What are your thoughts on the difference between being equitable and being fair?

29. What are the most important characteristics of a successful teacher?

30. Explain your grading philosophy.

31. When should a student fail a class or a school year?

32. If you have a student who would not do your assignment, how would you deal with the situation?

33. What do you want to see from students?

34. Why would you choose to teach in this school as opposed to another?

35. What would you most like to accomplish as a teacher?

Building Your Building © 2020 Solution Tree Press • SolutionTree.com
Visit **go.SolutionTree.com/leadership** to download this free reproducible.

Counselor Questions

Source: Adapted from American School Counselor Association, n.d., and schoolcounselor.com, 2019

Role of the School Counselor

1. What do you see as the main role of a school counselor?

2. What do you think is the most important characteristic of a school counselor?

3. What can you provide that is different from a social worker, school psychologist, or mental health counselor?

Strengths and Interests

4. What influenced you to be a school counselor?

5. What practical experiences have you had that make you feel capable as a school counselor?

6. What is your strongest asset?

7. How would you deal with cultural differences in a school setting?

8. What is something new you would bring to our program?

Foundation of Comprehensive School Counseling Program

9. How does a comprehensive school counseling program support the school's academic mission?

10. What is your school counseling and education philosophy?

11. What counseling theory or approach do you most closely follow? Why?

Delivery of Comprehensive School Counseling Program

12. What is your experience with implementation of a school counseling core curriculum?

13. How would you approach individual student planning?

14. How do you develop a positive relationship with students in individual counseling? Small-group counseling?

15. How would you handle a large group of students having attendance problems?

16. What experiences have you had with developing transition plans?

17. Describe how you would implement small-group counseling and classroom lessons.

page 3 of 7

Management of Comprehensive School Counseling Program

18. What type of school counseling activities would you institute to help close the achievement gap at our school?

19. What innovative and new ideas would you like to employ as a school counselor?

Advocacy

20. How have you advocated for students?

What Would You Do If . . .

21. One of your students tells you she is pregnant.

22. You suspect one of your students is being abused.

23. One of your students talks to you about wanting to kill himself or herself.

24. One of your students tells you he or she is being abused.

25. A student requests a teacher change because he or she doesn't like the teacher.

26. A parent requests you to switch his or her child's teacher.

27. A student requests to be in the same lunch period as his or her friend.

28. You suspect one of your students is abusing drugs or alcohol.

29. One of your students admits to being sexually active.

30. One of your students tells you he or she is gay.

31. One of your student's parents is terminally ill.

32. One of your students does not get into his or her first college choice.

33. One of your students wants to drop out of school.

34. One of your seniors is not going to graduate.

35. One of your students continues to fail mathematics (or any subject) each quarter.

Building Your Building © 2020 Solution Tree Press • SolutionTree.com
Visit **go.SolutionTree.com/leadership** to download this free reproducible.

Academic Coaches

Source: Adapted from Warren, 2018.

1. What makes you want to be an instructional coach?

2. Describe a time you led impactful professional learning.

3. Describe your education philosophy and how it helps you be an impactful coach.

4. Describe a time when you experienced pushback from a fellow teacher. How did you handle it?

5. How will you build a strong partnership with your principal to ensure teacher learning is effectively facilitated and leads to increased student achievement?

6. One of the primary areas of work for an instructional coach is to help teachers build their capacity and increase their ability to meet student needs. To accomplish this, an instructional coach must identify the essential components of quality instruction. With that in mind, talk to us in detail about what quality instruction looks like.

7. As a coach, how will you work to increase student achievement and close achievement gaps?

8. Teachers in our building have various skill levels and different needs regarding support and professional development. How will you determine the focus of your work and the strategies you will use when differentiating your work with adult learners?

9. Please discuss the skills and dispositions (personality traits) that ensure you are a successful instructional coach. Why are you the right person for this job?

10. Tell us one thing about yourself that we may not know.

Principal and Assistant Principal

Source: Adapted from American Association of School Personnel Administrators, n.d.

1. Please provide an overview of your professional experiences, describing the experiences you feel have prepared you for success in this role and have helped craft your vision for school leadership.

2. If you were hired for this position, what would you identify as your top three priorities for starting a new year with a new community for students and parents?

Building Your Building © 2020 Solution Tree Press • SolutionTree.com
Visit **go.SolutionTree.com/leadership** to download this free reproducible.

3. Please tell us about a time when you had to lead people through a controversial change. How did you handle this situation, and what would you do differently if you could do it over again?

4. A decision is made at a district administrative meeting regarding an instructional issue. You don't completely agree with the decision, in part because you expect there to be significant resistance at your school regarding implementation. How would you proceed?

5. What do you believe are your most outstanding contributions to your current district?

6. What do you believe are your greatest strengths as an administrator?

7. In what areas do you feel that you want to continue to grow?

8. What would the students at your current school say about you?

9. How do you manage the multiple responsibilities of an administrator?

10. What process do you use to solve problems and resolve conflicts between staff members?

11. A staff member comes to you saying she is having trouble collaborating with a teammate. The teammate is new and does not want to share ideas or discuss student data during team meetings. Instead, this colleague complains about the amount of meeting time and attempts to end the meetings as quickly as possible. What would you do?

12. How do special area courses (for example, physical education, art, or music) contribute to student achievement in general and to the attainment of core curriculum standards?

13. Our district serves many students from linguistically and culturally diverse backgrounds. What do you believe a school should offer bilingual students and their families?

14. What is important to keep in mind when providing services to students who qualify for bilingual services and who also have an individualized education program (IEP)?

15. With our district's focus on inclusionary practices, teachers are expected to develop meaningful, differentiated learning experiences for the full range of students in their classrooms (students with IEPs, English learners, average students, self-motivated students, quiet students, high-performing students, and so on). How will you know if a teacher is reaching all students, and how will you support a teacher who is struggling with this?

16. What kinds of supports would you offer a brand-new teacher to help him or her be successful?

Building Your Building © 2020 Solution Tree Press • SolutionTree.com
Visit **go.SolutionTree.com/leadership** to download this free reproducible.

17. What has been your role regarding both academic and functional or behavioral response to intervention (RTI)?

18. The mother of a special education student calls you upset that her child's behavior plan is not being implemented as written and, as a result, her child is receiving inappropriate consequences. What actions would you take?

19. Tell us about a time when it took longer than usual to build trust with a coworker or staff member. How did you eventually build that trust?

20. Tell us about one of your most challenging interactions with a parent and how you worked through it. After reflecting on that experience, what did you learn that will assist you in future interactions with parents?

21. What steps will you take to get to know the staff in your new school?

22. You walk by a classroom empty of students and see a teacher sitting at his or her desk crying. What would you do?

23. What is the most challenging situation you have faced as a school leader or professional? What did you learn from that experience?

24. How do you remain current regarding best practices and research in curriculum and instruction?

25. Describe your beliefs as they relate to student discipline.

References

American Association of School Personnel Administrators. (n.d.). Principal/assistant principal interview questions. Accessed at https://aaspa.org/principalassistant -principal-interview-questions on December 21, 2018.

American School Counselor Association. (n.d.). Possible interview questions for school counselors. Accessed at www.schoolcounselor.org/administrators /interviewing-school-counselors on December 21, 2018.

Hodges, T. (2012). Gallup's teacher applicant report and hiring date: TeacherInsight. Accessed at https://google.com/url?sa=t&rct=j&q=&esrc=s&source=web&cd=2 &ved=2ahUKEwj79vPm9_DgAhXH6YMKHbeuAvIQFjABegQICBAC&url=https %3A%2F%2Fwww.gallup.com%2Ffile%2Fservices%2F175979%2FGEC%2520HR %2520webinar%252010_30_13.pdf&usg=AOvVaw2AH5T_14wBGFa5lOk _5buG on March 7, 2019.

Schoolcounselor.com. (2019). Interview questions. Accessed at https:// schoolcounselor.com/professional-development/interview-questions on July 25, 2019.

Warren, F. (2018). 10 interview questions for a potential instructional coach. Instructional Coach Academy. Accessed at https://theinstructional coachacademy.com/index.php/2018/03/19/10-interview-questions-for-a -potential-instructional-coach on January 14, 2019.

Building Your Building © 2020 Solution Tree Press • SolutionTree.com
Visit **go.SolutionTree.com/leadership** to download this free reproducible.

REPRODUCIBLE

Interview Recording Form

Candidate: _____

Interviewer: _____

Interview Question	Notes	Score
1.		
2.		
3.		
4.		
5.		
6.		
7.		
8.		
9.		
10.		
11.		
12.		

Final Score: _____

Building Your Building © 2020 Solution Tree Press • SolutionTree.com
Visit **go.SolutionTree.com/leadership** to download this free reproducible.

Overall strengths the candidate brings to our school:

What feedback would you give the candidate?

Other feedback:

Building Your Building © 2020 Solution Tree Press • SolutionTree.com
Visit **go.SolutionTree.com/leadership** to download this free reproducible.

REPRODUCIBLE

Interview Panel Commitment Form

As a member of our selection committee, you are required to demonstrate the utmost professionalism during the interview process. This includes the following.

- Everything in the interview is confidential.

- Do not speak about the candidates or the interviews to anyone.

- Do not discuss the questions or the answers with anyone.

- Be respectful of all candidates.

- Ask only what is on the script.

- Be honest with your feedback and ratings (using the following rating scale for each answer).

Rating Scale

Rating	Description
1	Candidate shared information but did not actually answer the question.
2	Candidate answered the question, but the answer was generic.
3	Candidate answered the question and gave some examples to support the answer.
4	Candidate answered the question very well and gave detailed examples to support the answer.

I understand and agree to the importance of professionalism in this very important process for our school.

Name of Interviewer: _____

Signature of Interviewer: _____

Sample Questions for Reference Checks

1. Please confirm the candidate worked with you between these dates _____ and _____ as a _____.

2. Would you hire (or rehire) this candidate? Why or why not?

3. Did the candidate make a substantial, average, or below average contribution to your school community? Please explain your answer.

4. Describe the candidate's attitude on a regular basis. What was it like in a stressful situation?

5. What strengths will the candidate bring to our school?

6. What areas of development did you communicate to the candidate? How did he or she respond?

7. How would you describe the candidate's written and oral communication skills?

8. What was your greatest challenge in supervising the candidate?

9. How does the candidate handle conflict with coworkers or stakeholders (such as parents)?

10. Is there anything else you would like to share before we make our decision?

PART II

KEEPING GREAT TEACHERS

CHAPTER 3

Supporting New Teachers

*Teachers who feel encouraged and comfortable with
your support will stay with you in a positive climate of
learning. You deserve to have that kind of school.*

—Jan Richards

> *After four challenging years and the need to hire for several positions in the
> months leading up to the current school year, Principal James finally feels a
> bit of relief. Now she can settle in knowing that she has hired the best teachers
> to fill open positions in her school. However, she begins hearing comments that
> teachers do not feel supported. Both new and veteran teachers are complaining
> that the job is incredibly difficult, especially when they receive zero support
> from the principal.*

Support is an interesting concept to explain because it often means different things
to different people. One definition states *support* is "the degree to which employees perceive that supervisors or employers care about their global well-being on the
job" (Kossek, Pichler, Bodner, & Hammer, 2011, p. 292). Another definition states
supporting staff means "providing them with the right training, backing them up,
rewarding them for their work, supervising them properly and regularly, keeping
the morale high, and making sure they have whatever they need to do their jobs
successfully" (Nagy & Vilela, n.d.).

What's clear from these definitions is that support can come in many forms,
both through an employer's actions and through his or her words (O'Donnell,

2014). So, what kind of actions and what kind of words show support? In a school, principals can offer support to new teachers in a variety of ways, which we will cover in this chapter. In essence, we contend that support involves helping and encouraging teachers; we define *support* as being there for teachers and providing them with what they need to do their job well. Simply put, support is caring for teachers.

We also acknowledge the most important aspect of defining support for school leaders is knowing how teachers define it. If a principal's definition of support is not aligned with the teachers' definition of support, this disconnect can lead to frustration for both school leaders and teachers. A principal might think he or she is providing support, but it might not be the support teachers need or want, so teachers continue to feel as though they are in a precarious situation, without the support of their school leader. For example, as a principal, you may think you are supporting the teaching staff because you have an open-door policy—teachers know they can come to your office anytime they need to. But the teachers feel supported when the principal visits their classrooms for conversations. This misalignment can then lead to teachers feeling unsupported and the principal feeling frustrated.

Jan Richards (2007), an assistant professor of teacher education at National University in Ontario, California, illustrates this point in her study of teacher morale. She surveyed teachers and principals with the question, "What behaviors or attitudes can I demonstrate that will achieve these goals?" By goals, the author refers to teacher morale. Richards (2007) compiled a list of twenty-two positive principal behaviors for the survey. She then gave this list to a group of one hundred teachers with less than five years of experience and to a group of one hundred principals. Each group had the task of prioritizing which behaviors mean the most to them for improving morale. According to the survey, teachers prioritize the following two principal behaviors as most important: (1) respects and values teachers as professionals and (2) supports teachers in matters of student discipline (Richards, 2007). Principals, however, had a differently prioritized list, starting with "Encourages teachers to improve in areas of teaching practice and professional development." (Richards, 2007, p. 50). This demonstrates that although teachers and principals are aware of the importance of providing support, both groups may think differently about how to offer that support.

Throughout this chapter, we discuss why support for new teachers is important, the different types of support, and what areas of support principals should focus on to support new teachers. We then offer some strategies to help support new teachers.

The Importance of Support

About once a year, we survey our staffs to ask teachers what they need from us or what we can do to help them, and the number-one answer they provide is *support*. Author and researcher Richard M. Ingersoll (2001) finds that a major factor in teacher retention is the level of administrative support teachers receive. In another study, Ingersoll and University of California, Riverside Dean and Professor Thomas M. Smith (2004) conclude that multiple supports lead to more teachers staying in their schools and even more teachers staying in the profession. Another study (Podolsky, Kini, Bishop, & Darling-Hammond, 2016) concludes that lack of support is one of the top-five reasons why teachers leave the profession, but it also shows teachers who don't receive support are twice as likely to leave the profession than teachers who do receive support. We argue, then, that providing support is another critical influential factor in increasing teacher retention. If you want to build your building by retaining the great teachers you hire, you must support new teachers.

One reason providing support can increase teacher retention is because support helps minimize the stress new teachers face. We know how stressful teaching can be, especially for a new teacher. New teachers are trying to learn how to manage students and parents, work with colleagues, collect and analyze data, readjust their teaching strategies, meet the school and district accountability expectations, and so much more. Principal and school leader support can help make these new tasks seem less overwhelming.

In addition to being a very stressful job, teaching can also be a very lonely job; new teachers can feel isolated as they work in classrooms, by themselves with their students, behind closed doors. Support from school leaders can help new teachers feel connected, informed, and encouraged so they can do the job well. In addition, the principal can create that culture of support for new teachers through establishing an effective PLC and ensuring all new teachers are members of collaborative teams. If all new teachers are members of collaborative teams, that will minimize that feeling of being lonely and isolated when they have colleagues who they can depend on, collaborate with, and problem solve with.

Another reason support is tied to improved teacher retention is because of the amount of time new teachers spend at school. New teachers likely spend more time at school than anywhere else. Human resources consultant Michele O'Donnell (2014) argues, "Workers spend more time at their workplace with their co-workers than anywhere else in a work week, which means the workplace is where many employees look for support on a daily basis."

If principals increase teacher retention rates by supporting the teachers they hire, then it behooves them to re-examine their support strategies to ensure those strategies are effective. Let's first consider the types of support new teachers often require.

Types of Support

In the following sections, we will explore two types of support—(1) personal and (2) job related. We will define these types of support and discuss what events could lead to teachers needing each.

Personal Support

Every year in our work with educators, we encounter teachers going through significant events in their personal lives that could impact their work in schools. Such significant events can be positive or negative, which means they can cause either positive or negative stress. In fact, Hans Selye (1974), one of the original researchers on the topic of stress and known as the Father of Stress, distinguishes between *distress* and *eustress*. *Distress* is when a negative event causes a stress response; *eustress* is the stress response a positive event causes. Even if the stress is positive, it can still have a negative impact. For example, think about how distracted a person can be when in the middle of planning a wedding, before the birth of a baby, or while finishing up a degree of study. These distractions, although positive, take up a lot of time, which can result in feeling stress about getting the job done at work. Other times, it may just create stress because of all the responsibilities or tasks that accompany the positive event. Either way, whether in distress or eustress, teachers benefit from the support principals provide during that significant event.

Examples of negative personal events that can cause distress include the following.

- Diagnosis of a serious illness (self or loved one)
- Caregiving for aging parent
- Death in the family
- Marital or family issues
- Financial issues

Examples of positive personal events that can cause eustress include the following.

- Birth or adoption of a child

- Marriage

- Graduation or other life transition

- Milestone birthday

- Retirement

To provide support during these times, principals must first be aware of the events. Ideally, school leaders establish trusting and open working relationships so teachers feel comfortable sharing with the school leader if they are experiencing stress from a personal event. However, new teachers won't have such a relationship with school leaders. School leaders must take the time to check in with new teachers on a continual basis so these teachers have the opportunity to share personal events if they wish. Principals and other leaders need to show a genuine care and concern for their new teachers, listen effectively, and ideally possess some counseling skills, such as being able to probe and ask questions, paraphrase, show genuine interest in others, demonstrate empathy, and so on if they are to provide effective personal support.

Job-Related Support

If one thing is predictable about education, it is to always expect changes—from the transition of students from year to year to significant job-altering events, such as new district initiatives and changes in teaching assignments. These changes can significantly impact teachers. An American Psychological Association (2017) survey of 1,500 employees finds change in the workplace is not only linked to employee stress but also to employees thinking about leaving their workplace. If leaders know changes at the school can cause stress for teachers, they need to be aware of what those changes are, how the changes will impact teachers, and what emotional support teachers might require.

Examples of job-related change events include the following.

- When there will be a change in teaching assignment for the upcoming year and a teacher will be teaching something different or at a different level

- When a teacher must move his or her classroom into a new space

- When a teacher becomes a member of a different collaborative team (such as when a teaching assignment changes) or colleagues on an existing collaborative team change

- When teachers are told about expectations related to their job they have not heard before or been made aware of; for example, teachers must sign in on a computer system when they arrive in the mornings, or they must submit their collaborative team meeting notes to their administrator

- When there are changes to policies that require teachers to do things differently, such as changes in grading policies

Teachers can also require support for job-related issues not due to change. New teachers especially might struggle emotionally as they adjust to their new position and responsibilities. For example, new teachers find some peer-to-peer relationships to be a source of stress. New teachers might feel pressure to fit in, not let their colleagues down, or be held to the same standards as their colleagues. New teachers may also feel fear related to their new position for a variety of reasons. They might feel nervous about losing their new job if they don't perform well. As a result, new teachers may refrain from taking risks or asking questions. Another source of fear could be failure. New teachers might fear their students will fail, or they might have fear when having to face difficulties with parents.

New teachers often also need support related to challenges of their new position. For example, a new teacher may be struggling with how to find resources to support a lesson, or he or she could be struggling with student discipline issues. A new teacher may be experiencing stress about how to contact a parent to deliver unpleasant news about a student. He or she could be nervous about how to respond to a hostile email. These specific issues or challenges relate to the actual teaching duties and responsibilities of all teachers, but new teachers are facing them for the first time, including teachers who may not be new to the profession, but rather, new to the school. Principals can easily forget that many tasks all teachers do comfortably, for a new teacher, can naturally cause stress and uncertainty. Providing support to new teachers throughout the process of learning the job is essential. Understanding it will take time until new teachers feel confident and can work through their job-related challenges independently is just as important.

How a principal provides support—either personal or job related—will have a lot to do with the traits the principal has. Elaine K. McEwan (2003) describes ten roles that highly effective principals can take on, and all ten can help principals provide support to teachers.

1. Communicator

2. Educator

3. Envisioner

4. Facilitator

5. Change master

6. Culture builder

7. Activator

8. Producer

9. Character builder

10. Contributor

Knowing how important providing support is, we encourage principals to self-reflect and acknowledge their areas of strength and weakness in providing effective support to new teachers.

In the remainder of this chapter, we examine how the cultural landscape of the school goes far in promoting a supportive atmosphere for new teachers, we name and describe specific support areas school leaders should be aware of, and we provide strategies for supporting teachers in these areas.

Areas of Support

As a school leader, there are many ways you can structure and organize your school to ensure new teachers are receiving the support they need. We have identified specific areas you can focus on to increase your level of support for new teachers: school culture, job expectations, scheduling, evaluation, collaboration, resources, communication, classroom management, and new-teacher onboarding.

School Culture

The principal and other school leaders obviously play a key role in ensuring support for new teachers. The decisions school leaders make in offering support influence and shape the culture of the school.

We have already discussed the importance of creating a welcoming environment in chapter 1 (page 9) when marketing your school. The principal must ensure that a welcoming environment continues and remains as positive for teachers in the school as it is for those visiting. Front office staff often end up playing a critical role in the new teacher's experience. When new teachers need assistance with rules and procedures, need supplies, need to know where certain things are stored, and so on, the front office is often the first place new teachers go. As a result, ensure your front office staff know the role they play in supporting new teachers. Have frequent dialogue with the front office about how you expect staff members there to support the new teachers in the building.

The more staff members new teachers can turn to for information, the more support they will receive. This includes staff like custodians, another group that should be approachable for new teachers. For example, if a new teacher needs more desks for his or her classroom, does the teacher know who to ask? Does he or she feel comfortable and receive support from all members of the school community? Everyone in the building should be aware of who the new teachers are and ensure they are welcoming and supportive, especially during the first year. This means it is the school leader's responsibility to ensure these expectations are communicated with the rest of the staff in terms of the role they play in supporting new teachers. Arrange a time to introduce new teachers. Compile an information packet with the new teachers' pictures and some information about them to distribute to the staff. The purpose is twofold; first, to ensure everyone in the building is aware of who the new teachers are, and second, to ensure everyone knows their role in supporting the new teachers in the building.

In a PLC, staff and teachers are united in their belief that all students can learn at high levels (DuFour et al., 2016). This belief is part of the foundation of a school culture that values support, and every member of a PLC understands the need to work together toward the common goal of high levels of student learning.

Leaders can use the reproducible "Ten Team-Building Activities" (pages 82–83) to design fun ways to help build relationships and trust among staff.

Job Expectations

School leaders should be crystal clear about job expectations from the moment they advertise the vacancy, throughout the hiring process, and all the way until the new teacher is now officially working in their building. Specifically, school leaders need to be clear on what their expectations are for new teachers, including the instructional expectations (such as what they expect to see when they walk into the teacher's classroom, or expectations for how teachers plan their units or assessments). In addition, school leaders need to be clear on their basic expectations of teachers, such as dress code, protocol for being out sick, expectations for communicating with parents, and so on. The best way to do this is through the use of a faculty handbook. Every school should have an updated faculty handbook that clearly outlines all those expectations. Take some time to ensure your faculty handbook includes all the basic and major expectations and that certain components are not missing (see the reproducible "Sample Faculty Handbook Table of Contents" on pages 84–87 for an example).

Once the faculty handbook is created, updating the handbook should be a yearly task, preferably one done in collaboration with the school leadership team (this includes administrators, teacher leaders, department heads, and so on). We recommend school leaders go through the handbook with new teachers. Expectations can be overwhelming, and items that seem routine and self-explanatory to you can be confusing or unclear to new teachers. Offering support for expectations will ensure teachers know what is expected of them, which can help to alleviate the stress that comes with starting a new job.

Scheduling

Susan Moore Johnson (2006), the Carl H. Pforzheimer, Jr. Professor of Teaching and Learning at the Harvard Graduate School of Education, finds "misassignment is inequitably experienced by new teachers, who often are expected to teach classes or courses that are left over once experienced teachers have chosen their schedules" (p. 5). Which classes a school offers, how many sections are available, what levels, class sizes, planning times, and, of course, who teaches what, are critical decisions for a school leader. What is your process for deciding how teachers fit in this puzzle? How do you determine who teaches what classes? How do you decide what a new teacher's schedule is going to look like?

Scheduling is foundational to running a school. Always ensure your scheduling decisions are based on what is best for student learning, rather than making scheduling decisions based on tradition ("This is the way we've always done it!"). For example, the schedule should have time built in for teacher teams to collaborate during the school day so that new teachers have the support of colleagues during regular collaboration.

New teachers should be scheduled to teach in their area of expertise and passion, and principals must give careful consideration to their class sizes and the types of classes they assign. For example, if the more experienced teachers always get the classes with the high-performing students while the newer teachers get the classes with students who may present challenges, new teachers are being set up for frustration and potential failure. Or if principals assign experienced teachers to the classes they are certified in and love teaching, while the new teachers get classes they are not certified in, again those new teachers could face serious challenges beyond what they can handle. New teachers typically do not have the experience or confidence to work through the additional challenges of teaching something they are not certified in or passionate about, handling larger class sizes, or dealing with tougher teaching assignments such as having classes with higher number of students or students with behavior challenges. As Johnson (2006) observes:

> Many teachers receive unfair or inappropriate assignments—an out-of-field class, many course preparations, large classes, or an excessive student load. Any one of these can dampen teachers' enthusiasm and diminish their effectiveness and satisfaction. However, it is the newest teachers who typically experience these challenges in combination, and those who might have been highly effective in ordinary circumstances frequently find such trying work settings overwhelming. All too often, they leave their school or teaching in disappointment and disgust. (p. 6)

Evaluation

Typically, we have found in our experience that most teachers feel nervous when it comes to getting evaluated. This process can be particularly daunting for new teachers because they have never been through this process before and do not have the knowledge or background of what that process is like. Take time to explain your school's evaluation process and review the evaluation tool with new teachers. You can do mock evaluations to show teachers how you will use the instrument; for example, do an informal classroom visit with informal feedback. One study shows new teachers whose principals frequently visit their classrooms and give informal feedback have lower frustration and anxiety with the formal evaluation process (Angelle, 2006). But no matter what system or evaluation tool your school or district uses, school leaders should always be consistent with how they provide support to new teachers when it comes to evaluations.

Throughout the evaluation process, reassure new teachers that the evaluation tool is not a *gotcha* instrument, but rather a tool school leaders use to help teachers grow their skills with feedback. Every teacher, even veteran teachers, has room for growth. Authors Kendyll Stansbury and Joy Zimmerman (2000) stress that it takes time for teachers to learn the job and do it well. Although some graduates may come out of college as rock star teachers, many do not. Many need support and on-the-job training. Stansbury and Zimmerman (2000) go on to explain, "No one wants to see incompetent teachers in classrooms, but in this era of rising expectations, care must be taken that beginning teachers are not continually hired and then let go in the name of raising standards" (p. 11). Be patient with your new teachers; building your building requires investing time and energy into ensuring their success.

Collaboration

The support new teachers receive from colleagues is instrumental to their success. The Center on Educational Policy (Rentner, Kober, Frizzell, & Ferguson, 2016) finds that 60 percent of teachers report collaboration to be helpful to a great extent and that it is a good use of their time. Another study finds that teacher retention (and satisfaction) can be improved if school leaders foster a culture of collaboration (Kardos & Johnson, 2007). Another study looks at various initiatives to help retain new teachers, hoping to determine which factors are actually having an impact on keeping new teachers in the classroom (Ingersoll & Smith, 2004). The study finds one of the strongest factors for retaining teachers is when new teachers have a common planning time with other teachers in the same subject area and scheduled time during the school day to collaborate. Superintendent Derrick Meador (n.d.), who has written extensively about effective school leaders, argues the principal is the driving force in this collaboration. The principal must ensure a collaborative culture is deeply embedded in his or her school—not only to improve student achievement but also to help retain new teachers and ultimately help all teachers improve their practice so all students benefit.

One study compares new teachers who have access to collaborative environments versus new teachers who do not and finds that one in five new teachers (21 percent) who did not have access to collaborative teams actually left the profession after one year, while 18 percent changed schools (Ingersoll, Smith, & Dunn, 2007). It is the job of the school leader to ensure collaboration that focuses on the right work. Teacher teams should be collaborating regularly during time provided within the school day. New teachers who work in PLCs have an advantage when it comes to support through collaboration. The second big idea of a PLC is collaborative culture (DuFour et al., 2016). In a PLC, teachers engage in collaborative conversations about their goals, the curriculum, their strategies for ensuring students learn, and the results they achieve (DuFour et al., 2016).

Leadership researchers Kimberly Barraza-Lyons and Alesha Daughtrey (2011) find that PLCs have a positive impact on teacher retention. They also find that participation in a PLC is connected with longer retention, as new teachers share and discuss their practices, work together to reach a common goal, and feel less isolated. As a result, new teachers build on their experiences and continue to gain confidence and become better and better teachers. As new teachers see their students' successes, they become more confident. Creating a collaborative culture in your school certainly increases the likelihood of keeping your new teachers (Podolsky et al., 2016; Stansbury & Zimmerman, 2000). For teachers to participate in such a powerful process, the principal must ensure they are all on teams that focus on student learning.

Resources

It is no secret—teachers need a variety of resources to do their jobs effectively, from basic classroom supplies to instructional aids, books, and computers. Even veteran teachers continue to spend money out of their own personal budgets for their classrooms. Consider the financial burden that can put on a new teacher. David Nagel (2017), editorial director, education for 1105 Media's Public Sector Media Group, and editor-in-chief of THE Journal, reports classroom teachers spend an average of about $500 a year on classroom supplies. Specifically, 77 percent of teachers spend at least $200 a year while others can spend up to $5,000 a year (Nagel, 2017).

For a new teacher, who may have been unemployed for a while or who is straight out of college, having to spend money to purchase items for his or her classroom is additional stress principals should try to minimize or eliminate. If principals provide new teachers with needed resources, these leaders at least minimize one level of stress and maximize the chances of new teachers being successful.

We recommend every new teacher receive a new teacher kit. The kit should include a variety of resources. Suggested resources include the following.

- Basic classroom supplies (pencils, erasers, paper, tape, glue, stapler, ruler, calculator, hole puncher, dry-erase markers, whiteboard eraser, sticky notes, markers, scissors, clipboard, and so on)

- Resources for students (books, journals, tissue, hand sanitizer, snacks and prizes, a classroom set of whiteboards and dry-erase markers, and so on)

- Ideas for classroom design (bulletin boards, enrichment corners, learning centers, and so on)

- An "Advice to New Teachers" memo (see the reproducible on page 88), which includes tips every new teacher should know

- An updated list of websites that includes online resources for new teachers (see the reproducible "Websites for New Teachers" on page 89)

Teachers can store all these items in a bin in their classrooms or even in shoulder bags. In addition to taking the time to create a kit—and if you have the money— also give each of your new teachers a one-hundred-dollar gift card to purchase anything else they need or want on their own for their classrooms. If you are unable to do so, then enlist your parents and local businesses to donate certain supplies for classrooms so that teachers do not have to purchase them on their own.

Putting thought and effort into ensuring all new teachers have the resources they need to begin teaching demonstrates how supportive this new environment will be for them. With such support, new teachers can focus on actually preparing for teaching students. Good support increases the likelihood that new teachers will stay in the profession (Boogren, 2015; Stansbury & Zimmerman, 2000).

Communication

Sometimes principals expect new teachers to arrive as effective communicators with the skills to clearly express their thoughts and resolve any issues. Sometimes new teachers can struggle in this area, specifically in communication with colleagues, administrators, and parents. Being able to effectively communicate is a required skill for almost any job. It's through effective communication that we resolve issues, manage conflicts, speak up, build relationships, and so on, yet consider how much on-the-job training your school provides in these areas.

Teachers must communicate effectively both verbally and in writing. The school leader's role in supporting communication skills is to be proactive in ensuring new teachers are aware of the school's expectations and then provide support and coaching throughout the year on how to effectively communicate with a variety of audiences. Let's examine three audiences a new teacher could experience difficulty communicating with.

With Colleagues

How does a new teacher attempt to resolve a conflict with a veteran teacher? How does a new teacher handle negative communication he or she may hear from veteran teachers? How does a new teacher communicate respect for the years of experience a veteran teacher brings? Principals should address all these questions with new teachers to help them understand communication challenges they may face in their first year and how to overcome them. Brainstorm strategies together and be sure teachers have the tools they need to communicate well. For example:

- Communicate face to face.
- Use appropriate tone of voice.
- Listen.
- Know what you want to say.
- Be clear.
- Be respectful.
- Find a good time and location (the hallways are not a good spot to have conversations).
- Be mindful of body language.
- Be honest.
- Be open to feedback.

Most important, by having these discussions about communication at the beginning of the year, principals are setting the tone for new teachers to come to them for further support during the year if and when difficult situations with colleagues arise.

With Administrators

How should a new teacher communicate with an administrator if he or she disagrees with something or is struggling and needs help? Principals should take some time with new teachers to discuss how they want new teachers to approach them with any concerns they may be experiencing. We have always emphasized an open-door policy with new teachers (and all teachers); as school leaders, we were always available for open and free communication about concerns. New teachers especially need to know they are encouraged and welcomed to speak openly. In addition, we recommend principals provide opportunities for anonymous communication as well by setting up a mailbox or some kind of a location where new teachers can communicate their thoughts or concerns anonymously if they prefer. Principals are also encouraged to continue to hold one-on-one meetings with new teachers throughout the year to keep that communication ongoing.

With Parents

That first phone call to a parent to communicate a concern can be a difficult task for a new teacher. New teachers not only need guidance in this area but also sometimes a little coaching may help. Sit down with your new teachers and write an email together or make a parent phone call together. Our rule with parent communication has always been if it is an email, never write more than three lines. If the message takes longer than three lines to write, then you need to pick up the phone and call the parent. Encourage new teachers to always forward you any negative emails from parents so you can draft the response together or prepare a script together for a phone call. Prepare and role-play for those tough parent meetings beforehand. Terri Eichholz (2017) offers the following tips to new teachers for communicating with parents.

- Be proactive.
- Don't take it personally.
- Ask parents for advice.
- Get involved in the community.
- Choose your battles.
- Admit when you're wrong.

In addition, ensure that your own communication is clear about the use of social media as a communicative tool. What are you school's guidelines for using websites, blogs, Twitter, Facebook, and so on?

Classroom Management

New teachers and even veteran teachers new to your school typically have less experience with classroom management or have had very different experiences in their previous jobs that required a different set of skills. A Public Agenda (2004) survey finds that "more than one in three teachers say they have seriously considered quitting the profession—or know a colleague who has left—because student discipline and behavior became so intolerable" (p. 3). More recent reports demonstrate this still holds true. Teachers have been reported leaving the profession in high numbers, stating student behaviors as one of the main reasons (Behrman, 2017; Downey, 2015; Self, 2018). Teaching Tolerance (2016) administered a survey and found that 45 percent of teachers who said they wanted to leave the profession wanted to leave because of classroom-management concerns. In addition, the Public Agenda (2004) survey states "85 percent [of teachers] believe new teachers are particularly unprepared for dealing with behavior problems" (p. 3). As a result, school leaders must proactively ensure there is a tight schoolwide discipline policy that all teachers (and students and parents) clearly understand. For example, a schoolwide discipline policy with four simple steps, like those that follow, helps guide new teachers when dealing with classroom-management issues.

- **Step 1:** Verbal warning

- **Step 2:** Written warning and parent contact

- **Step 3:** Silent lunch detention and parent contact

- **Step 4:** Office referral and parent contact

As a school, decide how staff will proceed through the steps. How often will the steps reset so students have the opportunity to start from a clean slate and fix their behavior? We also suggest school leaders define the difference between *minor* and *major* infractions so teachers know what set of steps to follow (see the reproducible "Minor Versus Major Infractions" on page 90).

If your school has implemented other proactive discipline measures such as Positive Behavior Intervention Supports (PBIS), a schoolwide character-education program, or a privilege-based system (students lose privileges with infractions), ensure clearly articulated processes. Training for new teachers must include the school's discipline policy and any staff-implemented programs to help manage student behavior. School leaders must support new teachers as they work through their first year to determine what their classroom-management plan will be.

Also ensure new teachers have ongoing conversations with peers and administrators about ways to be proactive to minimize classroom disruptions and infractions. Talk often about how new teachers can build relationships with students, highlight and celebrate positive student contributions, and promote a positive learning environment. In other words, provide new teachers with tips and strategies throughout the year so they can build strong classroom-management skills. Do not assume new teachers will figure it out on their own; guide and support them along the way! The reproducible "Classroom Management: Tips for New Teachers" (pages 91–92) provides strategies for proactively managing the classroom.

New-Teacher Onboarding

New-teacher onboarding is when schools have created an induction program for new teachers. In others words, there is a thought-out, preplanned series of events that will provide support to new teachers all throughout their first year as a teacher (and sometimes even in their second year). A meta-analysis of fifteen studies examining teacher induction programs shows such programs consistently have a positive impact on teacher retention, classroom instructional practices, and student achievement (Ingersoll & Strong, 2011). All school leaders should carefully consider their new teacher induction programs to determine whether or not they are providing a positive impact. Induction programs should include an orientation and ongoing new teacher group meetings and mentoring, as well as planned professional development. (We address mentoring and professional development in chapter 4 on page 93 and chapter 6 on page 137.)

An ongoing onboarding program, where all new teachers meet with the principal and other key staff members to share information and continue dialogue, is another source of support for teachers. Meeting agendas could include operational items (for example, clarifying a procedure the faculty handbook outlines), sharing success stories and challenges, brainstorming ideas for instruction, and team check-in. The purpose of onboarding meetings is to provide support to new teachers so they have an opportunity to share and celebrate each other, gain ideas and strategies that will help in their classrooms, provide operational information, and address concerns they may be experiencing (such as stress) at that moment.

Look Ahead

If principals use multiple ways to support the new teachers in their schools, they have a better chance of building their buildings and keeping the teachers they hire. Principals and other school leaders create the conditions that make their schools supportive working environments or just places teachers will stop along the way before turning to a new career or finding a job at another school. In the next chapter, we discuss developing a mentoring program for new teachers. You will learn how to set up an effective mentoring program for your new teachers as another way that you can keep them in your building.

Next Steps

"Ten Team-Building Activities" (pages 82–83) provides some examples of activities to help build relationships and trust among your staff.

"Sample Faculty Handbook Table of Contents" (pages 84–87) shows the kinds of topics and sections you may want to consider for your faculty handbook. Your handbook should clearly outline expectations so teachers know what the school expects of them.

"Advice to New Teachers" (page 88) is an example of a memo for new teachers that provides advice as they begin their careers. We laminate (or print and frame) these tips and present them to new teachers.

"Websites for New Teachers" (page 89) is a list of websites new teachers can access for a variety of resources.

"Minor Versus Major Infractions" (page 90) shows how minor infractions compare to major infractions so new teachers are clear on student discipline behaviors considered minor (the teacher should handle) and behaviors considered major (the teacher should involve administrators).

"Classroom Management: Tips for New Teachers" (pages 91–92) is a handout for guidance on classroom management.

REFLECTION QUESTIONS

1. What strategies do you currently use to provide personal support to new teachers? How about job-related support?

2. What type of support is the hardest for you to provide? Why? How can you strengthen your skills in that area?

3. How can you create (or continue to strengthen) a collaborative culture in your school to ensure new teachers receive support from their colleagues?

4. How can you improve your school's or district's new teacher induction program?

Ten Team-Building Activities

Frozen T-Shirt Contest

Purchase plain white T-shirts. Roll up each separately and place each in the freezer for a few days. The day of the activity, organize teachers into groups. Each group gets a frozen T-shirt. The first group to thaw the T-shirt and have one group member put it over his or her clothes wins.

Board Games

Bring a variety of board games (Twister, Pictionary, Clue, and so on) into a large space (such as the gym). Divide staff into groups of three or four and set up game stations so each group can circulate to play all the games as a team.

Scavenger Hunt

Divide the staff into groups of two or three. Give each team a list of things to complete. Activities could include take a selfie outside the principal's office, take a picture of a specific spot in the school, create an art project in the art classroom, and so on.

School Trivia

Come up with twenty questions about your school's history. For example, Who was the first principal? What month do the staff celebrate the most birthdays? What year did our building open?

Team Mural

Divide the staff into groups of three or four, and give each team a small canvas and paint. Each team is to paint a picture that represents them. Hang all the canvases together in the front office to represent your staff.

Getting to Know You Through Candy

Place five different types of candy on a table, and ask teachers to pick one piece. After each teacher picks a piece, share the following list and ask teachers to respond to the prompts next to the candy they chose.

- Nerds—Your dream vacation
- M&Ms—All the places you have lived
- Gum—Information about your family
- Gummy bears—Favorite movie and why
- Kit Kat—Your pet peeves

page 1 of 2

Personality Activities

Conduct a personality assessment and carry out fun activities to demonstrate how each personality is different from others. For example, give each personality group a problem to solve to see how each group solves it such as Compass Points or True Colors.

Facts About You

Place several items in a bag (anything you see around the house such as paper clips, bookmarks, plastic utensils, and so on). Ask each person to pick as many items as they want from the bag. The number of items teachers pick from the bag is the number of personal facts they need to share with the team.

Speed Puzzles

Bring several puzzles (with fifty to one hundred pieces) and have each group work together to complete the puzzle quickly.

Show and Tell

Have teachers bring in something of value to them or something they are proud of. Give them one or two minutes to share what they brought and why.

Building Your Building © 2020 Solution Tree Press • SolutionTree.com
Visit **go.SolutionTree.com/leadership** to download this free reproducible.

Sample Faculty Handbook
Table of Contents

Building Your Building © 2020 Solution Tree Press • SolutionTree.com
Visit **go.SolutionTree.com/leadership** to download this free reproducible.

6.0 Instruction

6.1 Syllabus

6.2 Unit Planning

6.3 Grading and Recovery

6.4 Late Work

6.5 Intervention and Enrichment Period

6.6 Response to Intervention

6.7 Writing Strategy

6.8 Study Guides

6.9 Classroom Décor

6.10 Instructional Expectations

7.0 Meetings

7.1 Expectations

7.2 Collaborative Team Meetings

7.3 Faculty Meetings

7.4 Content Team Meetings

7.5 Grade-Level Team Meetings

7.6 PBIS Team Meetings

7.7 Leadership Team Meetings

7.8 Administrator Meetings

8.0 Supervision, Schedule, Routines, and Expectations

8.1 Morning Routine

8.2 Morning Duties

8.3 Afternoon Duties

8.4 Supervision

8.5 Help Sessions

8.6 Supervision of Before- and After-School Activities

Building Your Building © 2020 Solution Tree Press • SolutionTree.com
Visit **go.SolutionTree.com/leadership** to download this free reproducible.

Building Your Building © 2020 Solution Tree Press • SolutionTree.com
Visit **go.SolutionTree.com/leadership** to download this free reproducible.

Building Your Building © 2020 Solution Tree Press • SolutionTree.com
Visit **go.SolutionTree.com/leadership** to download this free reproducible.

REPRODUCIBLE

Advice to New Teachers

Welcome to teaching! Get ready to change the world as you impact students on a daily basis by preparing them for their future. As you do that, we want to share some advice, tips, and suggestions with you to help you have not only a successful first year but many more successful years after that.

1. **Maintain a work-home balance:** You'll be a better teacher if you always find time to relax and unplug on weekends and holidays.

2. **Never stop learning:** Always continue to learn about ways to engage your students using different instructional strategies, technology in your classroom, and so on.

3. **Ask for help:** Others may not know you are struggling. It's OK to be honest and ask for help because chances are everyone has struggled in the past.

4. **Be flexible:** You must have a plan, but realize that plan may not work out in the end. Be willing to change course as needed.

5. **Build relationships:** You should build relationships with students, parents, colleagues, and other school staff and administrators.

6. **Be positive:** Always be positive and refrain from engaging in negative conversations.

7. **Be organized:** Teaching is difficult if you are unorganized. Come up with a system to record parent calls, log student issues, keep track of data, and so on.

8. **Be ready for showtime:** When students begin entering the school, it's showtime! Leave your personal baggage and issues at home and put on your showtime face.

9. **Be confident:** There will be students and parents who may not like you or may complain about you. Treat everyone with respect, and have confidence knowing you are doing what is best for students.

10. **Have fun:** Enjoy your first year. Keep a journal; no matter how challenging, you will look back on your first year and treasure the memories.

Websites for New Teachers

Following are some websites that offer a variety of free tools, templates, resources, and ideas for use in the classroom, from decorating your classroom to constructing lesson plans. Some of these websites also allow you to connect with other teachers, and some offer some resources such as articles on a variety of topics you may find helpful, such as classroom management and writing effective assessments.

- **Education World:** *www.educationworld.com*
- **Educator's Reference Desk:** *https://eduref.org*
- **National Education Association, For New Teachers:** *www.nea.org/tools /for-new-teachers-articles.html*
- **PBS LearningMedia Indiana:** *https://thinktv.pbslearningmedia.org*
- **Teacher's Corner:** *www.theteacherscorner.net*
- **Teachers Net:** *https://teachers.net*
- **Teacher Planet:** *www.teacherplanet.com*
- **U.S. Department of Education, Office of Educational Research and Improvement, What to Expect Your First Year of Teaching:** *www2.ed .gov/PDFDocs/whatexpect.pdf*
- **U.S. Department of Education, Survival Guide for New Teachers:** *www2.ed.gov/teachers/become/about/survivalguide/index.html*
- **We Are Teachers:** *www.weareteachers.com*

Minor Versus Major Infractions

The teacher should manage *minor behavior infractions*, including the following.

- Disruptions
- Defiance
- Disrespect
- Inappropriate language
- Property misuse
- Horseplay
- Use of electronic devices
- Inappropriate display of affection
- Academic dishonesty
- Tardiness

The teacher should refer students who commit *major behavior infractions* to the office. These behaviors include the following.

- Cursing at staff
- Defiance
- Fighting
- Harassment and bullying
- Property damage and theft
- Drugs, alcohol, or tobacco use
- Weapons
- Bomb threats
- Arson
- Vandalism
- Skipping class
- Continuation of minor behavior infractions

Classroom Management:
Tips for New Teachers

Following are some tips that all new teachers can benefit from to begin the school year with a strong classroom-management plan.

1. Learn all your students' names.

2. Clearly articulate your classroom expectations, and spend time teaching them to your students.

3. Be consistent in enforcing classroom expectations.

4. Think of a nonverbal strategy to get students' attention (no shushing or yelling). Choose a strategy such as turning off the lights, playing (or stopping) music, clapping three times, counting down from three, and so on. Practice that strategy the first few weeks of school.

5. Create clear procedures in your class for things like where to turn in work, how to line up, where to get supplies, and so on.

6. Make a positive phone call to all parents within the first month of school.

7. Select five students each month to write positive cards for to mail home.

8. Create engaging lessons that allow students to be active learners instead of learners who listen passively to lectures.

9. Always begin each class with a warm-up. The minute students walk into the classroom, there should be an activity for them to engage in immediately. This should be a part of your classroom routine.

10. Eliminate down time. No student should have nothing to do.

11. Create a positive intervention plan in your classroom. Reward students with points for following rules. Give out prizes when students have earned a certain number of points.

12. Avoid reprimanding students in front of their peers.

13. Contact parents as soon as you can when you see behavior issues—do not procrastinate with parent contact.

14. Be approachable—and be aware of your facial expression. In other words, smile as much as you can rather than expressing anger or frustration.

Building Your Building © 2020 Solution Tree Press • SolutionTree.com
Visit **go.SolutionTree.com/leadership** to download this free reproducible.

15. Greet and welcome each student into your classroom.

16. Establish positive relationships with your students. Get to know them and their interests.

17. Praise and compliment your students as much and as often as possible.

18. Encourage student feedback.

19. Stay in control of your emotions; never respond out of frustration or anger.

20. Ask for help!

Building Your Building © 2020 Solution Tree Press • SolutionTree.com
Visit **go.SolutionTree.com/leadership** to download this free reproducible.

CHAPTER 4

Mentoring New Teachers

The delicate balance of mentoring someone is not creating them in your own image, but giving them the opportunity to create themselves.

—Steven Spielberg

> *Principal James is generally pleased with how the new teachers in her building are adjusting to their new positions and integrating with the school community. To assist them, she has been implementing strategies to provide both personal and job-related support. Despite this assistance, one new teacher, Logan Williams, seems to be having difficulty adjusting. Principal James knows that research suggests mentoring as a promising strategy for supporting new teachers, so she asks another teacher on Logan's team to reach out to Logan and ask how things are going. Principal James is looking to start an informal network of colleagues who can support the new teacher. While there will be a formal process for support in the form of a mentoring program, Principal James knows that encouraging an informal structure, especially since it hasn't grown organically yet, will be beneficial to a new teacher.*

The Cambridge Dictionary defines mentoring as "the act or process of helping and giving advice to a younger or less experienced person, especially in a job or at a school" ("Mentoring," n.d.). We personally like to define *mentoring* as working with and growing from the influence of someone you trust and admire as a professional and as a person. A mentor can be someone you know—a parent, sibling, friend, coworker, or boss—or someone you've never met, like an author, whom you admire and have learned from.

In education, the mentoring process matches veteran teachers with knowledge and expertise with new teachers who have less knowledge and experience. Mentors take the new teachers under their wing, so to speak, to provide support, motivation, and advice, cheering the new teachers on when celebrating achievements, and offering guidance when challenges arise. In addition, mentors help mentees discover new opportunities and continue to build their passion for teaching—something that, as we've discussed previously, can be difficult for some new teachers to maintain during the struggles of the first year.

Research identifies a mentoring relationship as an essential step for achieving success in academia, among other professions (Roche, 1979), especially during professional transitions (Bligh, 1999; Freeman, 2000; Grainger, 2002; Levy et al., 2004). A meta-analysis of 112 individual research studies finds mentoring has significant behavioral, attitudinal, health-related, relational, motivational, and career benefits (Eby, Allen, Evans, Ng, & DuBois, 2008). The role of a mentor is to encourage the personal and professional development of a mentee through the sharing of knowledge, expertise, and experience. The mentoring relationship is built on mutual trust, respect, and communication, and involves both parties meeting regularly to exchange ideas, discuss progress, and set goals for further development (Page, n.d.).

In a three-year research study, the Pennsylvania Institute for Instructional Coaching (n.d.) finds the following about coaching.

- Ninety-one percent of teachers coached regularly stated that coaches helped them understand and use new teaching strategies.

- Seventy-nine percent of teachers coached regularly said that their coach played a significant role in improving their classroom instruction and practice.

- Teachers who were regularly coached one-to-one reported that:

    - They made significant changes in their instructional practice.

    - Their students were more engaged in the classroom and enthusiastic about learning.

    - Attendance increased dramatically in their classes.

In addition, "the most effective professional development model is thought to involve follow-up activities, usually in the form of long-term support, coaching in teachers' classrooms, mentoring, or ongoing interaction with colleagues" (Ball, 1996).

Elena Aguilar (2017) explains that the key difference between mentoring and coaching in schools lies in the purpose for the support and the formality around the process. Coaching is far more formal than mentoring and has a more expansive end goal. Aguilar (2017) further explains coaching is professional development. Its purpose is to help an adult learner improve his or her practice—whether that is teaching or leadership. Therefore, coaching is far more structured than mentoring. Effective coaching is anchored in goals (the coachee's goals, the school's goals, and student goals). Formal agreements around meetings, confidentiality, and processes are established at the start of the coaching relationship.

Another benefit of mentoring programs is that mentors can play a major role in reducing employee turnover. Lucinda Gray and Soheyla Taie (2015) find the percentage of beginning teachers who are currently teaching is larger among those assigned a first-year mentor than among those not assigned a first-year mentor (92 percent and 84 percent, respectively, in 2008–2009; 91 percent and 77 percent, respectively, in 2009–2010; 88 percent and 73 percent, respectively, in 2010–2011; and 86 percent and 71 percent, respectively, in 2011–2012).

Researchers W. Brad Johnson, Gail Rose, and Lewis Z. Schlosser (2007) describe the following components as common in mentoring relationships.

- Mentorships result in enduring personal relationships.
- Mentorships are increasingly reciprocal and mutual.
- Mentors provide direct career assistance.
- Mentors provide social and emotional support.
- Mentors serve as models.
- Mentoring results in an identity transformation in the protégé or mentee.
- Mentorships offer a safe environment for self-exploration.
- Mentorships generally produce positive career and personal outcomes.

All of these components are incredibly important, especially in the field of education, because first-year teachers are expected to perform at the same level as a thirty-year veteran teacher. Education is one of the few professions where this happens; without strong mentorships, new teachers are more susceptible to failure and burnout.

The most important part of mentoring is building the relationship and committing to sharing knowledge and experience. Mentoring is beneficial to the mentor as well as the mentee. Being tasked with developing new teachers gives mentors a sense of fulfillment that helps keep them satisfied with their work.

Every new teacher has spent years in university classrooms learning from professors and many hours observing and student teaching, but not until new teachers actually step into their own classroom do they truly understand how much there is still to learn about educating students. Mentoring is critical to shortening the learning curve for new or inexperienced teachers, which we found means that new teachers can become much more productive in a shorter period of time.

In this chapter, we define two types of mentoring that occur in schools: (1) informal and (2) formal. We examine the characteristics that make a good mentor, the role of the mentor, components of an effective mentoring program, and strategies for success.

Types of Mentoring

There are two types of mentoring: (1) informal and (2) formal. Informal and formal mentoring are similar but have distinct characteristics.

Informal mentoring has very little structure and is based on the chemistry between the two partners in a mentoring relationship. Informal mentoring will sometimes even develop a long-term friendship between mentor and mentee. *Formal mentoring* is structured, is based on specific objectives and plans, is often measured, and brings people together based on need. A formal relationship typically lasts for a specified amount of time and then formally ends (although sometimes a mentor and mentee may decide to continue their mentoring relationship informally at that time).

University of Wisconsin educators Belle Rose Ragins, John L. Cotton, and Janice S. Miller (2000) compare informal and formal mentoring and conclude that both types are beneficial *if* the mentoring is highly satisfying for the mentee, and they argue that informal mentoring is better than no mentoring at all.

Informal Mentoring

While formal mentoring programs are important (and we would argue every school or district should have one in place), informal mentoring, where professional relationships develop organically between two people and where each gains insight, knowledge, wisdom, friendship, and support from the other, is important as well. Ragins and Cotton (1999) argue that informal mentoring is more beneficial than formal mentoring because informal mentors are more likely to engage in positive psychosocial activities such as counseling, facilitating social interactions, role modeling, and providing friendship.

As mentoring becomes more formal, research suggests that the level of interaction as well as the quality of information shared decreases (Johnson & Andersen, 2009), resulting in fewer long-term advantages for protégés, mentors, and organizations when compared to mentoring relationships that develop naturally and voluntarily.

Informal mentoring develops voluntarily because mentees and mentors readily identify with each other. The mentor has *been there and done that* and can help the mentee navigate situations in which he or she may need help. These relationships can last for years, usually with a friendship that grows into a relationship of learning and growing together.

Informal mentors provide more of several types of career-development functions, including coaching, providing challenging assignments, or increasing mentee exposure and visibility. One result of informal mentoring is that mentees are much more satisfied with their mentors than with formal mentors. These differences may be attributed to the underlying differences in the structure of the relationships. Mentees and mentors readily identify with each other. The mentor may see him- or herself in the mentee, and the mentee may wish to emulate the mentor's qualities. Finally, in informal mentoring, the mentee and mentor are selective about whom they wish to approach for a mentoring relationship (Nemanick, 2000). Informal mentoring is a strong and valuable tool for developing new employees. It is friendship first, learning and career second and third.

School leaders can set the stage for informal mentoring to happen by first having veteran teachers participate in the interview and selection process. We routinely have teacher teams interview new teachers and then watch them teach a class. This is very powerful because even in a short amount of time the teams start to bond and build relationships with the candidates. Since they participate and their input is considered when making the final decision, they almost feel an ownership to the process and are much more inclined to start building a relationship that usually starts as informal mentoring, but many times becomes a lifelong friendship.

We also have monthly team-building meetings and bimonthly social activities, such as bowling, cards, and dinner. There is no obligation to participate in the social activities, but the team-building activities are mandatory and a great way for the staff to get a better understanding of each other.

Formal Mentoring

Many schools and districts have formal mentoring programs to provide support for new teachers. Successful mentoring programs are key to preparing new teachers for the classroom and for retaining talented new teachers. Formal mentoring should be a comprehensive, coherent, and sustained process that takes place over several years. These programs include training for the mentor, thoughtfully matching the mentors and mentees specifically to their subject or grade level. Schools should all have collaboration time and personal plan time built into the day for teachers to learn together to increase their knowledge of best practices. In this chapter, we focus on formal mentoring structures. We begin with the characteristics and role of the mentor.

The Mentor

Regardless of the type of mentoring, mentors serve as *teachers of teachers*; therefore, mentors should understand research-based best practices and be able to articulate them to their mentees. An effective mentor tailors his or her support based on the mentee needs he or she observes. An effective mentor will take care of new teachers by listening, helping, and holding mentees accountable to grow and succeed.

The mentor must always be a positive role model, lead by example, and demonstrate professional behavior. Mentors can demonstrate their professionalism to the new teacher in the following ways.

- Keep information confidential.
- Show respect for all views.
- Treat others with kindness and respect.

- Admit when they are wrong.

- Follow through with responsibilities; don't overpromise or underdeliver.

A great mentor is like a coach. He or she encourages independent behavior but is still there to provide support. The mentor teaches managerial skills, especially for working with students. A great mentor will also provide specific feedback based on observed behaviors or actions. These combine to foster a relationship of trust, where the mentor can identify specific areas of growth for the mentee.

A mentor must both support and challenge. A mentor who is neither supportive nor challenging can create a barricade to growth, causing the mentee to enter an academic stasis. A mentor who is supportive but not challenging will confirm the status quo for the mentee rather than inspire advancement. A mentor who is challenging but not supportive will cause the mentee to retreat and withdraw. Growth and vision only occur with a mentor who is a combination of both (Bower, Diehr, Morzinski, & Simpson, 1999). A mentor typically becomes invested in the career progression and development of the protégé or mentee and often provides such essential functions as counsel, challenge, and support (Johnson & Andersen, 2009).

Following are some specific characteristics of mentors.

- **Inspirational:** An effective mentor will help inspire the new teacher to want to improve his or her practice. Mentors can inspire first and foremost by being a positive role model and setting clear expectations and goals while at the same time teaching how to reach those expectations and goals. Also, showing how to never give up on a student, even if that student has given up themselves, is significant.

- **Empowering:** When a mentor empowers the mentee, he or she helps the new teacher build confidence and strength in his or her abilities. Part of this is empowering the mentee to make good decisions. For example, when a mentee comes to the mentor for advice, one of the first things a mentor should ask is, "What are your thoughts?" or "How do you think you should handle the situation?" It is very empowering to give someone the opportunity to help them work through a problem. As much as the mentor may want to give the mentee the answer he or she feels is best, it is more empowering for the mentee to give his or her thoughts and ultimately work together to problem solve. The mentor should be careful not to enable the mentee, however. Mistakes are opportunities for learning.

- **Passionate and knowledgeable:** The mentor must be passionate and knowledgeable about best practices in teaching. Hattie's (2012) meta-analysis rates over 252 influences and effect sizes related to student achievement. The most influential factors include collective teacher efficacy (that the teacher has a belief that he or she can truly make a difference), response to intervention (RTI), common formative assessments, discussion, transfer of knowledge, and many more.

    In PLCs, the key to improved learning for students is continuous job-embedded learning for educators (DuFour et al., 2016); increasing adult knowledge will increase student knowledge. The mentor's role is paramount in helping the new teacher understand that teachers are always learning. The mentors would have an understanding of the systematic approaches to student learning that are part of the PLC process, which they in turn would share with their mentees. For example, how to create high-quality formative assessments and how to use the information from the assessments to drive instruction, intervention, and extensions.

- **Kind, supportive, and helpful:** The mentor must be kind but also willing to hold the mentee accountable to achieve agreed-on goals. A supportive mentor is available to listen and answer questions. A great way to listen and be supportive is when a mentee asks a question, the mentor's response should be to ask the mentee what he or she thinks about the issue. This forces the mentee to move past looking to the mentor for the answer and to look inward first to self-reflect.

- **Approachable:** A mentor must be friendly and easy to talk to. The mentee shouldn't feel hesitation about communicating with his or her mentor. This is why we recommend a peer, rather than a superior, act as a mentor. It is usually more comfortable for a new teacher to build a relationship with a peer.

- **Able to give constructive feedback:** It is important for the new teacher to see the mentor as nonevaluative; while at the same time, observe the new teacher on a regular basis.

Mentors can have different styles. An *instructive mentor* tends to direct the interactions while a *collaborative mentor* offers suggestions and solutions. A *facilitative mentor* poses questions to deepen thinking. There is a time and place for each style, and the mentor must know when to use each.

A good mentoring relationship is a two-way street; mentors are most effective when they have the qualities previously listed, but they can only be effective if mentees are open to feedback and have a reflective mindset for growth and improvement.

Effective Mentoring Programs

When building or implementing an effective mentoring program, we suggest school leaders take the following five steps.

1. Carefully match mentors and mentees.
2. Set clear expectations for mentees and mentors.
3. Support mentors.
4. Recognize mentors.
5. Continuously evaluate program effectiveness to determine where to make changes to improve the process.

Carefully Match Mentors and Mentees

There must be a process for selecting and matching the mentor with a new teacher. We have used an interest survey to see which new teacher has more in common with which mentors. In addition, take into consideration things like a gender match, common cultural backgrounds, close proximity of classrooms, similarity of work assignments, and so on. Also, consider what you want to accomplish. What skills does the mentee have that need more work? What strengths require less attention?

When we match mentors and mentees, we look for potential mentors who are skilled at building relationships and increasing student achievement. We look for mentors who are also organized and can clearly communicate procedures and processes that are important. This helps the new teacher start to learn the culture and how to navigate the school's established norms.

A mentor must have the skills and desire to be a continual learner. He or she must collectively define goals and expectations. If a mentor is not a good fit with a mentee, it is okay to declare a mismatch and rematch the mentee with a more suitable mentor.

Set Clear Expectations for Mentees and Mentors

It is important to set clear expectations for mentees. Leah Halper (2017) suggests the following for mentees.

- Take the initiative in the relationship. Invite your mentor to meet with you, suggest topics to discuss, and ask for what you need. Use email, phone, and in-person communication.

- Bring questions, concerns, and problems to your mentor, but also share successes and ideas. New faculty can bring many positive elements to the mentor-mentee relationship.

- Meet often; scheduling meetings in advance, being spontaneous, and a combination of the two are all fine, as long as the mentee and mentor agree with the approach.

- Be clear about what you need, and if an activity or suggestion isn't of interest, say so. Stick with teaching-and-learning, academic, community, and work-life-balance issues that are truly of interest to you.

- Don't expect your mentor to know everything or be able to help in every situation. But do check with your mentor early on when you need help.

- Ask for information and, when appropriate, advice.

- Be open to discussions and constructive alternative ways to handle teaching and professional responsibilities.

- Elicit a mentor's help in developing other informal supportive relationships.

- Be honest about any concerns regarding the mentoring relationship, even if they are minor.

Halper (2017) provides the following best practices and expectations for mentors.

- Respect your mentee's time. Schedule meetings as much as possible around his or her needs, and let go of expectations about how often you should meet.

- Listen much more than you talk.

- Avoid a deficiency mindset that's not supportive of what this new faculty member offers. Find out what your mentee is good at, passionate about, and working on.

- Address your mentee's needs as best you can. Offer more only when it's appropriate. Don't evaluate, rescue, or criticize.

- Provide help by serving as a learning broker, and be a sounding board for issues relating to the mentee's career goals and development.

- Provide suggestions and advice on goals and activities that might lead to rewarding opportunities, understanding that your mentee might enjoy different challenges than you do.

- Give feedback or advice tentatively, and only if asked directly. Respect that your mentee might not follow it. Suggest a second or third person's opinion, also, thus helping your mentee expand his or her network.

- Be a catalyst for your mentee developing his or her own network. Point to others he or she might reach out to and engage.

The reproducible "Calendar of Topics for Mentors" (page 110) provides a schedule of topics mentors and mentees can focus on during their meetings.

Support Mentors

We continually talk about supporting new teachers, but it is just as important to ensure we are supporting mentors as well. School leaders must support mentors by providing resources and time. One strategy we suggest is providing the mentors with a substitute quarterly for their classes so they can observe the mentee in practice and provide reflection and feedback. One of the most precious resources in education is time, and principals should always be willing to provide extra time to help develop new teachers. School leaders should also have a monthly meeting with the mentor and mentee to discuss their progress.

Recognize Mentors

Mentors usually perform their mentoring duties because they consider them a rewarding aspect of their profession. However, mentoring is a largely private endeavor, and often neither peers nor superiors are even aware of the workload mentors carry, let alone laud their efforts. Meeting on a regular basis with mentors is essential to a principal's responsibilities. Discuss and reflect on the mentoring process and the new mentee's progress. We have found that providing lunch and having a discussion is one of the most effective things leaders can do to recognize a mentor's contribution. Everyone loves to eat, and spending less-formal time allows conversation to grow organically.

Evaluate Program Effectiveness

As with any program, evaluating it to determine its effectiveness is valuable and necessary. How can we get better if we never evaluate what we are doing to see what is working well and what needs improvement? Evaluating a mentoring program is critical if we want to ensure it is doing what we want it to do. In other words, is your mentoring program truly supporting the new teachers in your building? Is it helping new teachers improve their practice? Is it producing the ultimate goal of helping to keep new teachers in your school or district? Think of what data you will collect and monitor to evaluate your program and how you will then analyze it and use that information to make changes.

The Resident Educator Program

The state of Ohio has a comprehensive mentoring program called Ohio Resident Educator Program (Ohio Department of Education, 2019). This process pairs a new teacher with a veteran teacher, who has gone through extensive training to be a mentor. This is a very formalized process focused on standards aligned to the state's teacher-evaluation system in seven areas: (1) students, (2) content, (3) assessment, (4) instruction, (5) learning environments, (6) collaboration and communication, and (7) professional responsibility and growth:

1. Students

    a. Gather and use information about student development, students' prior learning, and abilities to plan and deliver appropriate instruction.

     b. Build relationships with students by establishing and maintaining rapport, valuing each student as an individual, while avoiding the use of bias, stereotypes, and generalizations.

2. Content

     a. Use specific concepts, assumptions of learning, content-specific strategies, and skills in planning and instruction.

     b. Demonstrate an understanding of important grade-level content, concepts, and processes in the Ohio Academic Content standards and school curriculum.

3. Assessment

     a. Understand and use a variety of formal and informal assessment techniques to collect evidence of students' knowledge and skills.

     b. Identify learning standards, align assessments with curriculum and instruction, and communicate these clearly to students.

4. Instruction

     a. Set goals based on preassessment data, plan research-based instructional activities, and use appropriate and flexible grouping during instruction to support the learning needs of all students.

     b. Link the content to past and future learning, recognizing that the scope and sequence of learning activities must be differentiated to meet the needs of all students.

     c. Access appropriate materials, services, and resources, including human and technological resources to support instructional goals and meet students' needs.

5. Learning Environments

     a. Use strategies to promote respect, positive relationships, cooperation and collaboration among students.

     b. Use flexible learning strategies and grouping to engage students, foster curiosity, and encourage responsibility for their own learning.

     c. Transition between learning activities and use instructional time effectively.

6. Collaboration and Communication

    a. Use effective communication strategies in the classroom

    b. Use a variety of strategies for timely, confidential professional communication with parents, caregivers, colleagues, and other school staff.

7. Professional Responsibility and Growth

    a. Follow district policies, state and federal regulations, separating personal beliefs from professional interactions with students and families.

    b. Identify content knowledge, instructional strengths, and areas for professional growth, to develop and implement targeted goals, participate in relevant professional development, incorporating the new learning into instruction. (Ohio Department of Education, 2019)

Even though this formal process is specific to Ohio, anyone can use and adapt the standards because they are generally best practices. The following are tools mentors can use with mentees to help the process.

Data Measures Inventory

This tool is for recording and analyzing class demographics to give new teachers an understanding of the different needs of all their students. This inventory includes information such as number of students, ethnicity, male-to-female ratio, community type, student special needs, student language proficiency, previous student academic performance, and current student academic performance.

Synthesis of Student Data

This report gives new teachers an understanding of each student's differing learning needs. Each school or district can use its own data points; most use literacy levels, attendance data, assessment results, and discipline data to create a class profile.

Flexible Grouping Strategies

These strategies for grouping (and regrouping) students are based on assessments aligned to learning targets and group students specifically by what they know or don't know.

As leaders and in our work with schools, we are very strict in our requirement that teachers flexibly group their students; however, we are loose about *how* they flexibly group their students. (This is known as *loose-tight leadership*.) For example, our mathematics department uses formative assessments aligned to learning targets and then flexibly groups students based on the targets met or not met with different teachers.

Other teams of teachers in our school flexibly group students within their classrooms, where they design small-group lessons that allow students to relearn the targets in a different way than originally taught. Also, because there is a station for each target, the students take ownership of their learning.

Monitoring Student Learning

Teachers use formative assessments to plan for flexible grouping and then progress monitor and set goals to make sure students master the content. This part of the process is very important for new teachers to understand; slowing down and truly understanding where each student stands is more important than covering content.

Observations

Once the new teachers experience the planning process, getting to know students, and managing their classes, their mentors will start observations. When done well, such observations help new teachers with professional growth. They provide opportunities for new teachers to practice new skills, receive timely feedback, participate in collaborative conversations focused on instructional practices, and self-monitor progress, empowering and challenging themselves to be more effective. A simplified example of the observation process follows.

1. One-to-one preconference to discuss planning and what the mentor will observe during the class. The mentor will look for learning targets, instructional practices, formative assessments, and plans for flexible grouping based on the assessment information.

2. Observation (entire class period)

3. Collection of evidence (if necessary)

4. One-to-one postconference to determine the following and provide feedback.

   a. What was the purpose of the lesson?

   b. What evidence do you have to show that students understood?

   c. How will this lesson connect to new lessons, past lessons, and other content?

Such observations should be frequent—at least twice a month. They should provide the mentor and mentee with a view of the mentee's progress, growth, and areas in which he or she needs to improve. They also provide mentors and mentees with an opportunity to reflect and participate in conversations grounded in evidence to support growth and improvement.

School leaders should break this observation process down over several years so that feedback comes in manageable chunks. After the first year in this program, each mentee completes a self-assessment based on the seven standards from the Ohio Department of Education (2011) Resident Education Program. In collaboration with his or her mentor, the mentee will establish professional goals based on collected data and then develop an action plan.

Goals are an important part of this process. A goal should be SMART: strategic and specific (well-defined with a clear outcome and details); measurable (knowing when it will be achieved, using what measurement tool, and determining if it has been achieved); attainable (possible, and with clearly defined steps); results oriented (identifies who is responsible, who will provide support, and whether or not it aligns to school and district goals); and time bound (with a specific date set for achievement appropriate for keeping it on target; Conzemius & O'Neill, 2014).

Once the mentor and mentee collectively develop the goals and action plans, the mentee and mentor should monitor progress on a regular basis. These goals should be specific to the mentee's growth as a new teacher. Do not confuse these with team SMART goals that teachers set based on the progress of their students. Basically, the mentee will be setting goals around his or her progress as a teacher with his or her mentor and will also be setting team goals based on student learning within his or her collaborative team. See the reproducible "Mentee and Mentor Goal-Setting and Tracking Form" (page 111) for a process for setting and tracking goals.

Look Ahead

Being a new teacher is difficult. We believe the best way to work toward keeping your new teachers is to provide support, including a mentoring program. An investment in a systematic process to support new teachers results in happier teachers, more effective instruction, and, most importantly, students learning at high levels. We will further explore this idea of support in the next chapter, which focuses on the importance of leaders recognizing what teachers are accomplishing.

Next Steps

"Calendar of Topics for Mentors" (page 110) provides a schedule of topics for mentoring meetings with new teachers.

"Mentee and Mentor Goal-Setting and Tracking Form" (page 111) is a tool new teachers and mentors can use to identify goals as well as track mentee progress toward those goals.

REFLECTION QUESTIONS

1. What characteristics will you look for in mentors before assigning them to new teachers?

2. What activities will you plan for your mentors and new teachers?

3. What steps can you take to ensure your mentors actually support your new teachers?

REPRODUCIBLE

Calendar of Topics for Mentors

Month	Topic
August	• Participate in get-to-know-you activities. • Review school and district policies. • Review curriculum and standards. • Review classroom-management plan.
September	• Debrief about the first month: What went well? What didn't? • Discuss organization methods for certain tasks. • Practice writing positive emails and notes to parents.
October	• Discuss appropriate communication methods for parents. • Review student progress data.
November	• Review professional development needs. • Share professional development resources.
December	• Debrief about first semester: What went well? What didn't? • Set goals for the second semester.
January	• Review school and district policies relevant to the second semester. • Review student achievement data from the first semester. • Discuss needs for growth.
February	• Set up peer observations. • Share professional development resources.
March	• Discuss stressors of teaching so far. • Review solutions to minimize stress. • Discuss strategies for work-home balance.
April	• Collect evidence of success from year so far.
May	• Discuss advice for new teachers. • Review first year; celebrate successes.

Building Your Building © 2020 Solution Tree Press • SolutionTree.com
Visit **go.SolutionTree.com/leadership** to download this free reproducible.

Mentee and Mentor
Goal-Setting and Tracking Form

Purpose: To assist the mentee and mentor in establishing developmental goals.

Instructions: Mentee provides three goals to review with the mentor. Mentor identifies areas he or she may assist the mentee in growing over the course of their relationship. Example goals may include the following.

1. A personal goal associated with continuing education
2. A professional goal tied to building goals (such as increasing student achievement and closing achievement gaps)
3. A professional goal tied to professional development

Mentee SMART Goals and Development				
Specific Goal	Success Measure	Resources Required	Time Frame	Status and Comments

CHAPTER 5

Recognizing Teachers

Human nature demands recognition. Without it, people lose their sense
of purpose and become dissatisfied, restless, and unproductive.

—Ricardo Semler

> *With the mentoring program underway, Principal James knows the new*
> *teachers at her school are receiving a significant amount of support from*
> *both her and their mentors. Still, she spends a lot of time thinking about*
> *what else she can do to ensure new teachers want to stay. At a recent meeting*
> *with a veteran teacher, the conversation turned to the subject of appreciation*
> *and how the veteran teacher had left one of his first teaching jobs because*
> *he perceived a lack of recognition for his hard work and accomplishments.*
> *Principal James asked the veteran teacher if he felt she had implemented a*
> *strong recognition program. He replied with an honest answer: the principal*
> *could do more. After he left, Principal James began to think about how she*
> *could strengthen the recognition at her school so that all her teachers (the new*
> *and the veteran) felt appreciated and valued.*

The HR Council (2018) defines *employee recognition* as the "acknowledgement of an individual or team's behavior, effort and accomplishments that support the organization's goals and values." The Human Capital Institute (2009) defines *recognition* as "acknowledging or giving special attention to employee actions, efforts, behavior or performance" (p. 5). When applying these definitions to education, we also identify the need to acknowledge or celebrate teachers for their efforts or behaviors that ultimately help improve student achievement.

Throughout this chapter, we will discuss why recognition is important, forms of recognition, characteristics of effective recognition, and barriers to recognition. We then offer practical ways for you to recognize teachers in your school.

Recognition and Job Satisfaction

To understand why recognizing teachers is important, we first look at five theories that explore factors, such as recognition, that lead to job satisfaction. Why is job satisfaction so important? Research finds that job satisfaction leads to increased retention rates (Davies, 2001; Perrachione, Rosser, & Petersen, 2008; Terera & Ngirande, 2014).

One of the first theorists to make a connection between workers and recognition was Elton Mayo, an Australian-born psychologist, industrial researcher, and organizational theorist, in the 1920s (Gillespie, 1991). In his famous Hawthorne Experiment, Mayo predicted that by changing employees' working conditions, their performance would change; however, his experiment showed something completely different. Mayo found that attention from managers actually impacted employee performance more than working conditions, including salary (Gillespie, 1991).

Behaviorist B. F. Skinner's (1938) theory of operant conditioning argues that positive reinforcement of a certain behavior promotes repetition of that behavior. Then, Maslow (1943) introduced his theory of human motivation, with his pyramid of the five needs necessary for motivation and satisfaction. The fourth level, esteem and accomplishment needs, is where we see the need for recognition. If you recognize employees, they are likely to have higher satisfaction with their jobs.

In 1959, psychologist Frederick Herzberg publicized his motivation-hygiene theory, sometimes also called the two-factor theory (Herzberg, Mausner, & Snyderman, 1959). In his study, Herzberg interviewed several workers and asked them what satisfied and dissatisfied them about their jobs. He placed all those factors into two categories. The *motivators* or *satisfiers* are factors that lead to job satisfaction. One example is recognition (other examples include advancement, achievement, and so on). The *hygiene* or *dissatisfiers* are factors that lead to job dissatisfaction (such as work conditions and salary). Herzberg (Herzberg et al., 1959) states the absence of dissatisfiers does not automatically lead to job satisfaction; however, the mere presence of the dissatisfiers can lead to job dissatisfaction. In other words, having poor working conditions can lead to job dissatisfaction, but having good working conditions does not necessarily mean workers will be satisfied. However, the mere presence of satisfiers does lead to job satisfaction. Therefore, in the workplace, leaders can gain higher satisfaction levels "by introducing a recognition program" than they can "by supplying ever-higher employee benefits, which produce only marginal effects on job recognition" (Fisher, 2015, p. 35).

In 1964, Yale School of Management Professor Victor H. Vroom (1964) shared his expectancy theory, which states that a worker's motivation is a product of three factors: (1) expectancy, (2) instrumentality, and (3) valence. *Expectancy* refers to the degree workers think their efforts will end with a certain level of results. *Instrumentality* is the workers' perception of whether or not his or her success will lead to those results. *Valence* is the degree of satisfaction workers receive from those results. For some workers, those results may be a pay raise, and for others it could be recognition. Managers, therefore, should ensure their workers believe increased efforts will lead to results, and managers should reward those results in a manner that has value to each worker.

In summary, these five theories relate to job satisfaction and how leaders can improve either worker productivity or job satisfaction based on certain factors, many of which include recognition. We can conclude one of the reasons recognition is vital to retaining new teachers is because the theories demonstrate the importance of recognition to increase job satisfaction. And we know through research there is a strong positive correlation between job satisfaction and employee retention (Davies, 2001; Perrachione et al., 2008; Terera & Ngirande, 2014).

Despite these theories, statistics show recognition is seldom at the forefront of organizational leaders' minds. Results of a study titled *The State of Employee Recognition in 2012* (Bersin & Associates, 2012) include the following.

- "Only 17 percent of respondents report that their organization's culture supports recognition" (p. 9).

- Seventy percent reported being recognized once a year or not at all, even though "87 percent of organizations reported that their programs are designed to recognize service or tenure" (p. 9).

- Organizations with excellent recognition programs "experienced 31 percent lower voluntary turnover than those organizations with poor programs" (p. 10).

The *Trends in Employee Recognition* report (WorldatWork, 2013) notes, "Only 12% of organizations provide some training on recognition to managers . . . Nearly half [46 percent] of respondents believe senior management views recognition as an investment rather than an expense" (p. 5).

Aberdeen Group's (2013) report *The Power of Employee Recognition* finds:

> The greatest barrier to employee recognition programs in 2012 was the lack of senior executive buy-in. Today [2013], organizations struggle to gain manager buy-in, which can directly impact the time and resources dedicated to these efforts. . . . Only 14 percent of organizations provide managers with the necessary tools for rewards and recognition. (p. 2)

This same study (Aberdeen Group, 2013) finds the best way to improve employee engagement is through employee recognition programs, and the majority (60 percent) of "Best-in-Class organizations stated that employee recognition is extremely valuable in driving individual performance" (p. 1). There is clearly a disconnect between what organizational leaders know they have to do and what they actually do in terms of recognition.

Recognition and Retention

Recognition is absolutely critical in helping leaders retain teachers. Authors Barb Wingfield and Janice Berry (2001) discuss the three Rs of employee retention: respect, recognition, and rewards. Recognizing employees can lead to increased retention rates within the organization, including schools. In fact, the number-one reason Americans leave their jobs is because they do not feel recognized (Lipman, 2019; Rath & Clifton, 2004). Specifically, in one study (Andrews, 2011), teachers report when they were given recognition, they not only stayed in their schools but also felt motivated to continue to work hard. Given these findings, it is important for principals and other school leaders to consciously create a working environment that systematically recognizes teachers. If we know recognition leads to a higher probability that teachers will remain in their positions, then why would we not invest some of our time and energy into creating this kind of a working environment? When we spend time and energy selecting and hiring the best teachers for our school, we need to then do what we can to ensure they stay. Recognition is something that truly needs to be done for everyone in the building so we can ensure all our teachers continue to stay.

Forms of Recognition

Education writer Gary Gordon (2004) says principals set the tone, culture, and working conditions in their schools. He further states that in order to do this effectively, one strategy is to always recognize teachers' achievements by celebrating their successes (Gordon, 2004). Following are types of recognition—ways for leaders to celebrate the successes of teachers.

Public Versus Private

School leaders can choose to recognize teachers either in a public or private setting. Public recognition, of course, occurs in front of an audience of (most likely) peers, parents, or students. This type of recognition could take place, for example, during an assembly, in a newsletter, during morning announcements, on social media, and so on. With private recognition, leaders recognize teachers without an audience. Some examples of private recognition include emails, personal notes, or just a one-on-one conversation.

Top Down Versus Peer to Peer

When principals, department heads, or others in supervisory positions recognize a teacher, it is considered *top-down* recognition. The power to give recognition and how to give it is completely in the leader's control. Top-down recognition can be very meaningful to employees since it is coming from someone higher in the power hierarchy, sometimes a person who is in a position to hire, fire, and promote. *Peer-to-peer* recognition is when teachers recognize other teachers. Leaders must set up the structures to encourage and support peer-to-peer recognition. An example of peer-to-peer recognition includes putting a system in place where teachers can nominate other teachers for a recognition (this could be done through a voting system or a nominating system). Another example could be to provide an opportunity for teachers to give shout-outs to each other. It is interesting to note that in an American Psychological Association's Center for Organizational Excellence (2014) employee recognition survey, younger employees (ages eighteen to thirty-four) support the concept of peer-to-peer recognition more than their older counterparts (ages thirty-five to forty-four).

Individual Versus Team

Leaders or peers can recognize teachers individually or as a team. When recognizing teachers individually, leaders or peers give the credit and praise to the teacher who earned it. One study actually investigates the effects of individual recognition of a single team member and finds there is actually spillover effects on the person's teammates (Li, Zheng, Harris, Liu, & Kirkman, 2016). However, recognizing an entire team for its' efforts or actions promotes a collaborative culture. An effective approach could be to have a balance of recognizing teams as well as individual teachers.

Brooks Mitchell (2013), professor emeritus at the University of Wyoming and founder of Snowfly Performance Incentives (https://snowfly.com), outlines the *75/25 rule*. This rule proffers that a well-balanced recognition program will incorporate recognitions for individuals 75 percent of the time and teams 25 percent of the time. This is similar to the recognition athletes typically receive; the best teams win championships, but then individuals receive awards for the most valuable player or for the best player in a particular position. There is a balance between both forms of recognition.

Formal Versus Informal

Formal recognition is when there is a structure or procedure in place to give out recognitions and can include, for example, retirements and teacher-of-the month celebrations. Formal recognitions are typically based on a time frame, as these recognitions are planned. Formal recognitions are common in schools. However, they are not as effective in isolation because they occur infrequently; very few people receive them. *Informal recognitions*, on the other hand, are unplanned recognitions such as a thank-you card or an announcement during a faculty meeting. In an International Public Management Association for Human Resources survey in both the United States and Canada, 47 percent of respondents felt the formal recognition programs were effective, while 62 percent felt the informal recognition programs were effective (as cited in Saunderson, 2004). We believe frequent informal recognitions combined with formal recognitions (that already exist in most schools) can help strengthen the effectiveness of recognition programs.

Leaders should choose the form of recognition based on what those being recognized desire. We encourage you to survey your staff (including new teachers) to determine how they prefer to be recognized. (See the reproducible "Recognition

Survey" on pages 130–131.) In addition, reflect on your current recognition programs and practices. Determine what you do well and what recognition practices need improvement. (See the reproducible "Self-Reflection of Current Recognition Practices" on page 132.)

Characteristics of Effective Recognition

Once leaders determine the types of recognition their staff find most desirable, they should consider the following questions about the characteristics of effective recognition.

What Are You Recognizing?

For recognition to be effective, you must know exactly what you are recognizing. Are you recognizing teachers' results, efforts (even though they may not have produced results), or just a teacher because he or she brings something positive to the school or team, such as a good attitude or great work ethic? Researchers Jean-Pierre Brun and Ninon Dugas (2008) outline four recognition practices that will help strengthen the teacher recognition program in your school.

1. **Existential recognition:** Teachers are recognized for themselves and things unrelated to teaching. For example, recognizing a milestone such as a marriage, birthday, retirement, having a baby, and so on.

2. **Recognition of work practices:** Teachers are recognized for their job performance, such as for their teaching, supervision, classroom-management skills, and so on.

3. **Recognition of dedication to work:** Teachers are recognized for going above and beyond in their level of commitment. For example, volunteering to sponsor a before- or after-school club, offering time to facilitate extra help sessions for students, going to student games and activities, volunteering to sit on various school committees, and so on.

4. **Recognition of results:** Teachers are recognized for the results they produce, such as the results of an assessment, a survey, and so on.

Who Are You Recognizing?

Identifying who to recognize is another essential characteristic of effective recognition. This can be easily done when leaders know their teachers well and have built positive working relationships with them. Author, consultant, and employee loyalty specialist Cindy Ventrice (2009) notes, "People want you to know something about them before you choose how to recognize them. They are especially impressed if the recognition is unique and especially selected for them" (p. 151). To make recognition individualized, Ventrice (2009) suggests first identifying how each teacher contributes to your school, then finding out how he or she likes to be recognized, and finally, recognizing him or her in a personalized manner. Relationships play a big part in making an impact with recognition. Leaders should know teachers so when it is time to recognize them, they can do it in a way that is meaningful. Leaders can get to know teachers by having one-to-one conversations (both formal and informal), initiating conversations in the hallway, asking about weekend plans and family, providing a poll or survey, having an open-door policy, participating in social gatherings (leaders arrange) inside and outside of school, knowing which teachers are going through personal hardships, facilitating team-building activities, and so on. These are all examples of how leaders can invest in building relationships with teachers so when they do recognize a teacher, that recognition is that much more meaningful because it is personalized.

When Are You Recognizing?

For recognition to be effective, it has to be timely. When you see something worthy of recognition, recognize it right away! Best-selling author and employee engagement expert David Sturt (2015) compares this approach to recognition at the Olympics. Think about the winners—the International Olympic Committee recognizes each winner with a medal right away, not weeks or months afterward. If leaders recognize teachers immediately, more teachers will be recognized more frequently. Don't wait for a formal meeting or the end-of-year celebration to formally recognize teachers; instead, create frequent recognition opportunities throughout the school year. As Sturt (2015) suggests, "Don't wait for the 'right' moment, but rather help create moments that build a culture of appreciation and great work" (p. 59).

A Gallup poll (as cited in Hodges, 2015) asked more than 25 million employees around the world, including over 100,000 educators, about their workplace. One of the questions respondents rated the lowest was this item: "In the last seven days, I have received recognition or praise for doing good work." Only 29 percent of the teachers in this survey said they "strongly agree" with this statement (as cited in Hodges, 2015). If leaders incorporate more recognitions more frequently, the recognitions will have a stronger impact on teachers, and ultimately on the school culture and teacher retention.

Why Are You Recognizing?

Take the time to explain why you are recognizing teachers. Simply saying, "Good job!" is not really recognition. It is much easier to make such general statements, but for the recognition to be effective, it must be specific. "Vague recognition that could apply to anyone doesn't leave people feeling recognized" (Ventrice, 2009, p. 133). One great way to make the recognition meaningful is to tie it to the school's mission statement or goals. If your school's mission statement is to ensure the success of every child, then outline what specifically a teacher did that advanced this mission. The Human Capital Institute (2009) states effective recognition programs should tie the recognition to the organization's specific goals. If a program doesn't, it will have no positive impact whatsoever. Some schools have recognition committees to identify the kinds of behaviors, efforts, and results worthy of recognition. The committee then shares the list with the entire staff so everyone knows the standards for recognition. Indeed, "When you play a game, you want to know the rules before you begin" (Ventrice, 2009, p. 116). Therefore, ensure your recognition is specific, connects to your mission or goals, and, even better, meets those predetermined standards for specific behaviors, efforts, and results.

How Are You Measuring?

One last feature of an effective recognition program is to include a measure of accountability. There are two forms of accountability you want to identify. The first is principal accountability for effectively recognizing the teachers in the building. Have you established and outlined a schoolwide teacher recognition program that you then ensure is carried out? Roy Saunderson (2004), chief learning officer at Rideau Recognition (https://rideau.com), believes principal supervisors (superintendent, school board, and so on) need to have accountability built into their principal evaluation systems to ensure principals have outlined clear recognition programs in their schools.

The second measure of accountability is to assess the recognition program. Is it working or not? How do you know? Give staff surveys, have conversations, and examine staff retention and satisfaction data. This information can also help you revise your recognition program as needed so that it best meets the needs of all teachers, especially the new ones.

We now know employee recognition is important; it directly impacts the workplace culture and, ultimately, employee retention. We have explored the different forms of recognition and the characteristics. But with the many demands principals and other school leaders have, it can be incredibly difficult to actually engage in effectively recognizing new teachers and veteran staff members.

Barriers to Recognition

We both can admit that regular and targeted recognition has never been our strength—especially early in our careers as principals. There are several barriers that prevent principals from recognizing teachers as much as they should. For school leaders, recognition is often not a priority, or they want to be fair and not constantly recognize the same outstanding staff members. Leaders might not pay enough attention to teacher accomplishments to know what to recognize, or they themselves might feel unhappy in their job or for personal reasons, which impacts their ability to recognize others. Other leaders might not understand how to recognize teachers, or they might see themselves as too tough to have time for such fluffy pursuits as recognition. In the following sections, we share some barriers to recognition.

Other Priorities

A major barrier for implementing a recognition program is time (Branham, 2005; Kouzes & Posner, 2002; Nelson, 2012). There are never enough hours in the day for school leaders to get the job done. So, good principals and school leaders prioritize tasks. Teacher recognition often does not seem that important compared to the other tasks leaders have in the day, which means they never get around to it. Leaders often take for granted when new and veteran teachers are just doing their jobs. However, what may seem like normal accomplishments to seasoned school leaders are actually huge accomplishments for the teachers.

One solution to this challenge is to create an easy way to make recognition a part of a leader's everyday work. For example, creating a bank of simple recognition notes that are quick to adapt to different situations is one way to fit showing appreciation to teachers into a busy schedule. (See the reproducible "Bank of Simple Recognition Notes" on page 133.) In addition, create some simple certificate templates you can fill out and give to teachers throughout the year. Certificates are easy and simple to use for different recognitions, and teachers can keep and hang these certificates in their classrooms.

A Focus on Fairness

Every school has a handful of teachers who are *rock stars*. These are the teachers who always go above and beyond—they volunteer for everything, are great team players, have excellent relationships with parents and students, always have a positive attitude, and so on. Recognizing these teachers is easy because they do so much for the school. One of the barriers to recognizing these teachers is that leaders become afraid to recognize the same teachers all the time, running the risk of playing favorites (Branham, 2005; Kouzes & Posner, 2002). As a result, leaders try to be fair by recognizing everyone in turn. However, then it becomes too much trouble to find reasons to recognize everyone, so leaders stop recognizing altogether.

Leaders should remember that newer teachers need more recognition (they are just starting out in their careers), and it's OK to give them more. However, that doesn't mean it's OK to forget about veteran teachers. A solution is to create a documentation system that tracks the recognition you give to ensure you are balancing the recognition. (See the reproducible "Faculty and Staff Recognition Tracker" on page 134.) This tracking system can help you be aware of who you are recognizing so you are not always recognizing the same people. Although it is easier to see the rock stars, everyone contributes in some way to your school. You may just have to look harder to see the contribution so you can recognize it.

Lack of Attention

Leaders may not be paying enough attention to what teachers are doing to give them the recognition they deserve. Running a school is a big job—think about how many people are in your building and how many departments you are responsible for; it can be difficult to know what every person in the building is doing. Leaders can become too focused on the task instead of the people, so they can miss out on the contributions new and also veteran teachers are making in the schools

(Branham, 2005). How do leaders give recognition when they may not know who did what?

A solution to this barrier is to enlist an administrative assistant (or teacher leaders or team leaders) to keep track of new teachers' accomplishments, and then he or she can communicate that information to you. In addition, one of the responsibilities of teacher leaders or team leaders could be to report teacher accomplishments worthy of recognition.

Personal Issues

When you are unhappy or dissatisfied in your job, it becomes difficult to recognize others. The job of the school leader is always evolving, and a high stress level is far too common. Stress impacts your ability to see things beyond the immediate stressors and emergencies. This permeates throughout every layer of the organization, resulting in a whole school of unhappy people. The American Institute of Stress (n.d.) states that stress can impact our emotions, mood, and behavior. This impact of stress can profoundly affect how school leaders do their job, which includes interacting with teachers.

A solution for school leaders is to control their stress level by trying to understand what causes the stress, what relieves stressors, and then engaging in those activities. Stress-relieving activities include hobbies such as gardening, reading, painting, and exercising. Others include spending time with family and friends, going to the movies, shopping, and so on. Find what helps you relax and de-stress, and then engage in those activities. Otherwise, stress levels will only continue to make your job harder to accomplish, and the possibility of recognition more elusive. Education World (2015) outlines thirty strategies for principals to help reduce stress. Some of these strategies include:

- Make time to laugh.

- Listen to music.

- Make a *praise file* (a collection of all the positive emails and cards you get) and refer back to it whenever you need a feel-good moment.

- Spend time with students.

- Take the weekend off.

Not Knowing How to Recognize

It can be difficult to recognize new teachers because leaders simply do not know how (Branham, 2005; Nelson, 2012). How many leaders actually spend time planning all the different ways they can recognize teachers? When the school year begins and leaders become busy with the day-to-day responsibilities, it becomes difficult to engage in tasks they do not know much about. If recognizing people does not come to you naturally, it will be difficult to recognize your teachers.

The solution we advocate is to create a system with a time line that identifies all recognition methods and plans recognitions month by month. (See the reproducible "Yearlong Recognition Program, Month-by-Month Example" on page 135.) Such a plan takes out the guesswork and ensures this important task doesn't get left behind in favor of other priorities.

A Focus on Tough Leadership

Leaders sometimes mistake recognizing teachers as weak leadership or something for the "warm-and-fuzzy types, not for serious and performance-oriented managers" (Kouzes & Posner, 2002, p. 315). This obstacle may require leaders to change their personal understanding of what it means to be a good leader and accept that good leaders recognize their teachers. Director of Research for Gallup's Education Practice Tim Hodges (2015) notes, "Research shows that great principals create great workplaces for their teams and that recognition is a key driver of great workplaces. Further, teachers value principals who create a culture of recognition above almost any other issue."

Leaders with this mindset must familiarize themselves with the research supporting recognition and the impact it has on employee retention. They must make a commitment to best practice in this area in the same way they would with best practices for instruction, professional learning, or any other issue in education.

Strategies for Recognizing Teachers

Here we offer some practical strategies for recognizing new and veteran teachers alike. We have used these strategies in our own schools or observed other principals use them with their teachers. Implement a wide variety of strategies to create a well-balanced recognition program in your school. Be sure to share the details of the recognition program; for example, include a section in the school's faculty handbook that outlines the program.

- **Teacher of the month:** Each month, the teachers and staff vote for a teacher of the month and a staff member of the month using an online polling tool like Survey Monkey (https://surveymonkey.com). Announce the winners at a Friday staff breakfast and post their pictures on a bulletin board.

- **Monthly staff appreciation breakfasts:** Every last Friday of the month, staff and teachers receive breakfast the administration (or business partners) provides.

- **Newsletter staff highlights**: Each week, an administrator highlights a teacher or staff member for his or her achievements in the weekly school newsletter.

- **Kudos:** One day a week, encourage all teachers and staff to send various kudos about their colleagues to the front office. Compile and publish these kudos on the principal's blog every week.

- **Pass the trophy:** End every monthly department meeting with *passing the trophy*—where a staff member names a colleague for this award. The recipient keeps the award for the month, and then the following month, he or she names someone else in the department for it.

- **Positive cards:** Make cards available in the mailroom for all teachers and staff to write positive notes to their colleagues and place in their mailboxes.

- **Appreciation days:** Appreciation weeks for faculty and staff align with the U.S. calendar, but make your own appreciation days. As a team, honor the commitment and hard work of individuals. For example, students can write cards and letters, make posters, and so on. Create a calendar at the beginning of the school year that lists the dates and the teacher team responsible for organizing the recognition. The administrative team is responsible for Teacher Appreciation Week. (See the "Appreciation Days List Template" on page 136.)

- **Retirement breakfasts:** Retiring faculty and staff members receive recognition in celebration of their service to the school.

Present each retiree with a gift as well as a scrapbook commemorating his or her career.

- **New teacher celebration:** Celebrate the new teachers at the end of their first year with a breakfast or luncheon. Present each with a scrapbook of memories from his or her first year.

- **Welcome cards and breakfast**: Send a card to the home of every teacher, welcoming him or her back for the new school year and inviting them to a welcome-back breakfast.

- **Thank-yous from former students:** Ask former students to write thank-you cards or letters to teachers at your school.

- **Birthday cards:** Give teachers birthday cards. Someone on staff arranges the birthday cards in chronological order at the beginning of the school year, and they get passed around so everyone signs them as birthdays come up.

- **Donut delivery:** Once a month, have donuts delivered on a cart to teachers' classrooms.

- **Social media recognition:** Post recognition regularly on school social media (Twitter, the school website, Facebook, and so on).

- **Bulletin boards:** Dedicate a bulletin board to recognizing teachers. It should be in a prominent location so staff, parents, and students can all see it.

- **Certificates:** Give certificates to teachers when they demonstrate great results (such as the highest student achievement, lowest number of students failing, showing the most improvement, and so on).

Recognition in PLCs

In PLCs, where teams are working collaboratively, there is a natural venue for public and peer-to-peer recognition. Colleagues can recognize each other during collaborative meetings (formally or informally) almost on a regular basis. Recognition can be a simple acknowledgement of an accomplishment in the classroom that week or for completion of collaborative tasks, such as creating the common assessments for the unit.

Since PLCs are results oriented, teams focus on the results of their work, instead of their intentions. When those results show successes in student achievement, team members should naturally recognize and celebrate those wins through peer-to-peer recognition. In addition, the principal should also recognize and celebrate those wins through top-down recognition.

When collaborative teams meet goals in a unit or when teams show gains in student achievement, we recommend using public recognition to let other teams know success is possible. This can be done frequently because in a PLC, collaborative teams examine results constantly. For example, when common formative assessments occur frequently, teams analyze data frequently, allowing team members to determine if they have reached success or not. As DuFour et al. (2016) note, "Regular public recognition of specific collaborative efforts, accomplished tasks, achieved goals, team learning, continuous improvement, and support for student learning reminds staff of the collective commitment to create a PLC" (p. 221). They go on to state that recognition in a PLC allows leaders to say, "Let us all be reminded and let us all know again what is important, what we value, and what we are committed to do. Now let's all pay tribute to someone in the organization who is living that commitment" (DuFour et al., 2016, pp. 222–223).

Look Ahead

The theories and research clearly articulate the need for recognition in the workplace to help keep employees. If we want teachers to remain in our schools, we must create a culture of recognition where leaders and peers recognize one another in multiple ways through multiple formats. Recognition is an effective strategy to improve teacher retention rates, so as a principal, take the time to invest in creating a recognition program that has the elements mentioned throughout this chapter. We will now take a look at the impact professional development can have on retaining teachers. We need to not only recognize teachers but also develop them and grow their skills by providing them with opportunities to learn and become stronger teachers.

Next Steps

The "Recognition Survey" (pages 130–131) is a way to get input from teachers and staff about how they like to be recognized.

The "Self-Reflection of Current Recognition Practices" tool (page 132) is a questionnaire or graphic organizer school leaders can take to reflect on their current recognition practices.

"Bank of Simple Recognition Notes" (page 133) contains sample recognition notes school leaders can use to give to teachers when they do something worthy of recognition.

The "Faculty and Staff Recognition Tracker" (page 134) is an example of a documentation system to track the recognitions to ensure you have a well-balanced recognition program.

"Yearlong Recognition Program, Month-by-Month Example" (page 135) is example of a recognition calendar. You can use this template to create your own calendar to plan your recognition events throughout the year.

The "Appreciation Days List Template" (page 136) is a tool to organize the dates of appreciation days throughout the year and to note what team is responsible for celebrations.

REFLECTION QUESTIONS

1. How would you convince another principal about the importance of teacher recognition?

2. What forms of recognition do you currently use in your school? Are they effective?

3. From the five characteristics of what makes an effective recognition program, which one will be most difficult for you to implement? Why? How can you work through that?

4. Of all the barriers explored in this chapter, which of them makes it difficult for you to recognize teachers in your school? How can you overcome that barrier?

5. What is one way you can improve your school's recognition program after reading this chapter?

Recognition Survey

In an effort to create a well-balanced recognition program in our school, we would like your feedback. This information will help us improve how our school recognizes all our faculty and staff members.

After reading each statement, select *strongly agree*, *agree*, *disagree*, or *strongly disagree*.

Name: _____

	Strongly Agree	Agree	Disagree	Strongly Disagree
I am satisfied with our current recognition program.				
I feel recognized and valued.				
I prefer to receive recognition publicly.				
I prefer to receive recognition privately.				
Receiving recognition from my principal is more meaningful.				
Receiving recognition from my colleagues is more meaningful.				
I enjoy having our whole team recognized.				
I enjoy individuals being recognized.				
Recognition that is formal (structured and with a criteria) is more effective.				
Recognition that is informal (spontaneous and unplanned) is more effective.				

Please indicate your preferred method of recognition. Rank each one from 1–5, with 1 being your most preferred approach to being recognized.

_____ Verbal thank-you

_____ Written thank-you in an email or card

_____ Publicly in a staff meeting

Building Your Building © 2020 Solution Tree Press • SolutionTree.com
Visit **go.SolutionTree.com/leadership** to download this free reproducible.

_____ Publicly in a newsletter, on Twitter, Facebook, and so on, that goes to all stakeholders

_____ A certificate or token that can be treasured

Please rank, in order of importance, what you think is worthy of teacher and staff recognition with 1 being most worthy of recognition and 4 being least worthy of recognition.

_____ Being great at something (classroom management, technology, and so on)

_____ Going above and beyond (sponsoring a club, volunteering to stay late, and so on)

_____ Student achievement or accomplishment (such as students excelling on a test)

_____ Personal milestones (birthdays, marriages, and so on)

I would prefer recognition:

_____ Daily

_____ Weekly

_____ Monthly

_____ Annually

_____ Spontaneously—whenever it is earned

In the following space, please share any suggestions and strategies we can implement to improve our faculty and staff recognition program in our school.

Building Your Building © 2020 Solution Tree Press • SolutionTree.com
Visit **go.SolutionTree.com/leadership** to download this free reproducible.

Self-Reflection of Current Recognition Practices

Review your current recognition practices, and identify each type of practice. This will give you an idea of what kinds of recognition practices you will need to add to create a well-balanced recognition program. For example, if the majority of your recognition practices are public, you may need to add some private practices. If the majority of your practices are top down, you may want to consider adding some peer-to-peer practices.

Recognition Practice	Public Versus Private	Top Down Versus Peer to Peer	Individual Versus Team	Formal Versus Informal

1. What type of recognition does your school do well?

2. What type of recognition does your school need to improve on to have a more well-balanced recognition program?

Bank of Simple Recognition Notes

Recognizing a Teacher for Resolving a Concern With a Parent

I really appreciate how you worked through the issue with the parent. Your excellent problem-solving skills helped to resolve the parent's concern, and he or she left satisfied. Thank you for handling it in such a professional manner.

Recognizing a Teacher for Mediating a Student Conflict

Thank you for mediating between the two students who have been having issues for a few weeks now. I so appreciate how you took time to help the students come to an understanding that will hopefully now allow them to focus in class.

Recognizing a Teacher for Organizing a Field Trip

You did such a great job organizing the field trip for our students. What a great time everyone had! Our students made memories and had such an incredible experience—because of you. Thank you for putting in all the extra hours to make this field trip a reality for them.

Recognizing a Teacher for Raising the Most in a Fundraiser

Your class won for bringing in the most money during our school fundraiser! That happened because of your leadership and your commitment to our school. Your school spirit is so appreciated! The students had fun with your competitiveness, so thank you for making such a big difference for our school.

Recognizing a Teacher for a Great Lesson

That was an unbelievable lesson I just saw! It was clear how much time you spent planning for this lesson. The students were all very engaged and participated from beginning to end. Your passion for teaching is so evident. Our students are so lucky to have you as their teacher!

Recognizing a Teacher Team for Excellent Collaboration

I thoroughly enjoyed sitting in on your collaborative time today. Your discussion about the strategies you plan to try for struggling students was excellent. It is clear you all are dedicated to working with all our students and committed to do whatever it takes to help all students be successful. I look forward to seeing how successful the strategy ends up being!

Recognizing a Teacher for Completing the First Semester

You did it! You successfully completed your first semester of your teaching career. I have enjoyed watching you grow and work through all the challenges most first-year teachers face. Your professionalism and dedication to our school and students are so appreciated. You're off to a great start. I look forward to a great second semester. As always, I'm here for support should you need anything.

REPRODUCIBLE

Faculty and Staff Recognition Tracker

Teacher or Staff Member Being Recognized	Date of Recognition	Recognition Received

Building Your Building © 2020 Solution Tree Press • SolutionTree.com
Visit **go.SolutionTree.com/leadership** to download this free reproducible.

Yearlong Recognition Program, Month-by-Month Example

Month	Planned Recognitions
June and July	• Cards mailed home to every teacher with a personalized note and an invitation to breakfast
August	• Welcome-back breakfast • Certificates given to teachers and teacher teams with highest test scores from previous year and most improved test scores from previous year
September	• Donut delivery to all teachers
October	• Secret Santa peer-to-peer recognition—everyone selects a person he or she will recognize all month long through cards, emails, and so on
November	• Thanksgiving thank-you letter to teachers from the principal
December	• Personalized gift to each teacher (an ornament, framed staff photo, and so on)
January	• Certificates given to teachers and teacher teams with lowest class failure rates
February	• Donut delivery to all teachers
March	• One-to-one thank-you meetings between the principal and teachers
April	• Thank-you letters given to teachers from their former students
May	• Teacher Appreciation Week; treats given to teachers each day during the week • Celebration for retiring teachers

Ongoing Throughout the Year

- Monthly staff breakfast; recognize teacher of the month
- Monthly peer-to-peer recognition through passing the trophy
- Weekly staff recognition in the newsletter
- Weekly peer-to-peer recognitions through school blog or cards
- Cards or thank-you emails
- Social media recognition of teachers (Twitter, school website, and so on)

REPRODUCIBLE

Appreciation Days List Template

Appreciation Days	Dates	Teacher Team to Organize Appreciation
Public Safety Day		
Custodial Worker Appreciation Day		
Bus Driver Appreciation Day		
Counseling Appreciation Day		
Social Worker Day		
Paraprofessional Day		
Media Specialist Day		
Secretary Appreciation Day		
Teacher Appreciation Week		
School Nurse Day		

CHAPTER 6

Implementing Professional Development

There is no end to education. It is not that you read a book, pass an examination, and finish with education. The whole of life, from the moment you are born to the moment you die, is a process of learning.

—Jiddu Krishnamurti, Philosopher

> *As Principal James continues to reflect on her school year, she thinks about the great teachers she hired. She works hard to ensure they stay in her school by supporting them, recognizing them, and providing mentors for them. One very important component she also realizes her new teachers need is professional development. They do not necessarily have all the skills and tools necessary to effectively do their jobs.*

The Teaching and Learning International Survey defines professional development as "activities that develop an individual's skills, knowledge, expertise and other characteristics as a teacher" (Organisation for Economic Co-Operation and Development, 2009, p. 49). Linda Darling-Hammond, Maria E. Hyler, and Madelyn Gardner (2017) go a step further and define effective professional development as "structured professional learning that results in changes in teacher practices and improvements in student learning outcomes." Hayes Mizell (2010) states that professional development can actually refer to various work-related educational experiences:

Doctors, lawyers, educators, accountants, engineers, and people in a wide variety of professions and businesses participate in

professional development to learn and apply new knowledge and
skills that will improve their performance on the job. (p. 3)

Mizell (2010) goes on further to say that professional development can be either
formal (for example, conferences, workshops, and so on) or informal (for example,
discussion with a colleague, reading, and so on).

The need for professional development has increased—just think about how
drastically the teaching profession has changed since you were a first-year teacher.
Like school leaders, teachers are responsible for doing so much more now. Teachers
must close the achievement gap, increase achievement for students with disabili-
ties and for students whose first language is not English, analyze and utilize data
to make instructional decisions, implement research-based instructional strategies,
and so on—all while addressing classroom-management issues, student behavior,
and so forth. Teachers are held accountable for increasing student achievement for
all students. With all that is expected of teachers, it is critical schools and districts
provide professional development opportunities to all teachers—but especially new
teachers. There are so many reasons as to why this is essential.

- **Acquisition of knowledge:** An obvious reason why professional
  development is so important is because it is a way for new teachers, as
  well as veteran teachers, to acquire knowledge about current research.
  For instance, as a new teacher, Jasmine attended a PLC workshop with
  her principal. This opportunity provided insight about shaping her
  teaching practices to help all students learn at high levels and is what
  started her on a journey of learning with PLC transformation.

- **Inspiration for ideas:** Sometimes a professional learning opportunity
  may not result in learning new content, but instead, it provides
  practical ideas of how to put that learning into practice. For example,
  leaders can offer professional development on the importance of
  classroom management; however, providing specific ideas and
  examples of how to create a classroom-management plan is typically a
  lot more helpful for teachers.

- **Professional networking:** Through these learning opportunities, new
  teachers connect with other new teachers and veteran teachers, and
  they learn from each other's experiences. Professional development
  then becomes not just about learning new content or getting new

ideas, but about making friends and creating and strengthening a professional network of colleagues.

- **Student achievement:** Ultimately, the purpose of everything we do in education is to ensure all students learn at high levels. If new teachers are given valuable professional development, and, as a result, they gain knowledge, they take ideas back into their classrooms and create a professional network that they can call on whenever needed. When this happens, students benefit.

- **Retention:** Perhaps the most important reason to offer professional development is that it helps with teacher retention, which is what we are trying to accomplish in an era in which teachers are leaving the profession at a faster pace than they are entering it (Hope, 1999; Mizell, 2010). Really, retention is a benefit that comes from the combination of all of the benefits we mention in this list. When new teachers gain knowledge, are exposed to new ideas, are supported by colleagues, and have more tools at their disposal to increase student achievement, they are more likely to stay in the profession. In fact, Sam Brill and Abby McCartney (2008) note that research has found that "improving teachers' work environment and professional development are more cost effective and influential in convincing teachers to remain" than moderate salary increases (of less than 20 percent; p. 750).

If leaders are trying to increase retention rates for new teachers and teachers in general, it is imperative to re-examine how we support teachers in the area of professional development. How do leaders succeed in providing effective, meaningful professional development to help teachers learn, grow, and develop as professionals? To answer this question, we look at some theories on adult learning.

Theories on Adult Learning

Now that you know why professional development is so important not only for teacher retention but also for improving teacher quality and therefore student achievement, you want to ensure the professional development opportunities you provide are effective. In order to do that, we will study some of the theories on adult learning. As you prepare and plan to offer professional development in your schools, keep these adult learning theories in mind to maximize the impact of the learning opportunities you provide to your teachers.

Andragogy

The andragogy theory states that adults learn differently than children. Malcolm S. Knowles (1973) describes pedagogy as the art and science of teaching children and andragogy as the art and science of teaching adults. He believes the following four concepts about adult learners.

1. **They have a unique self-concept:** As children become older and more mature, they become less dependent and more self-aware and therefore self-directing. Thus, adults identify with an adult role. "Any experiences that they perceive as putting them in the position of being treated as children," Knowles (1973) states, are "bound to interfere with their learning" (p. 45).

2. **They learn from experience:** Experience becomes an adult's biggest resource for learning and provides him or her with a basis to relate all new learning to. As a result, andragogy theory of adult learning states there should be:

   > Increasing emphasis on experiential techniques which tap the experience of the learners and involve them in analyzing their experience. The use of lectures, canned audio-visual presentations, and assigned reading tend to fade in favor of discussion, laboratory, simulation, field experience, team project, and other action-learning techniques. (Knowles, 1973, p. 46)

3. **They learn for new roles:** This aspect of the theory states that adults are ready to learn when they take on new specific roles. Children learn things because they have to, but adults learn things they need to learn as they take on new roles in life. For example, a new medical student needs to have direct experience with hospitals, patients, and practicing doctors before he or she is ready to learn facts about pathology, anatomy, biochemistry, and other content (Knowles, 1973).

4. **They need to apply learning immediately:** Adults need to apply what they learn immediately in order for the learning to be effective, as opposed to students, who are learning what they need to know for the future.

Experiential Learning Theory

David A. Kolb and Ronald E. Fry (1975) explain four specific stages of learning in experiential learning theory that can help leaders plan professional learning experiences.

- **Stage 1: Concrete experience (feeling)**—This is where the adult is exposed to a new experience or situation.

- **Stage 2: Reflective observation (watching)**—The adult goes through a reflective observation where he or she reflects on that new experience.

- **Stage 3: Abstract conceptualization (thinking)**—The reflection results in new learning for the adult.

- **Stage 4: Active experimentation (doing)**—The adult applies the new learning to his or her environment.

According to Kolb and Fry (1975), effective learning only occurs when the adult has gone through all four of the stages in order. However, the adult learner can enter the cycle at any stage but then must follow it through in that order to complete all four stages.

The second part to this theory explains how adults learn best. Kolb and Fry (1975) explain two continuums: processing (how we approach a task) and perception (how we think or feel about the task). The continuum between stage 1 (concrete experience) and stage 3 (abstract conceptualization) is the perception continuum because stage 1 is the *feeling stage* and stage 3 is the *thinking stage*. The continuum between stage 2 (reflective observation) and stage 4 (active experimentation) is the processing continuum because stage 2 is the *watching stage* and stage 4 is the *doing stage*.

Based on the continuums and the four stages of learning, Kolb (1984) introduces four learning styles. (See figure 6.1, page 142.)

1. **Diverging:** This learner's dominant learning style is feeling and watching. This adult likes to look at things from different points of view and therefore would enjoy activities such as brainstorming.

2. **Assimilating:** This learner's dominant learning style is thinking and watching. This adult will take information and analyze it and put it in

logical categories; therefore, this learner would enjoy lectures and read-
ings if given time to think through the learning.

3. **Converging:** This learner's dominant learning style is thinking and
    doing. This adult likes to solve problems and make decisions and would
    therefore enjoy simulations, lab experiments, and practical applications.

4. **Accommodating:** This learner's dominant learning style is feeling and
    doing. This adult likes to learn from hands-on experiences and would
    therefore enjoy working with others to get work done and test different
    ways to get projects completed.

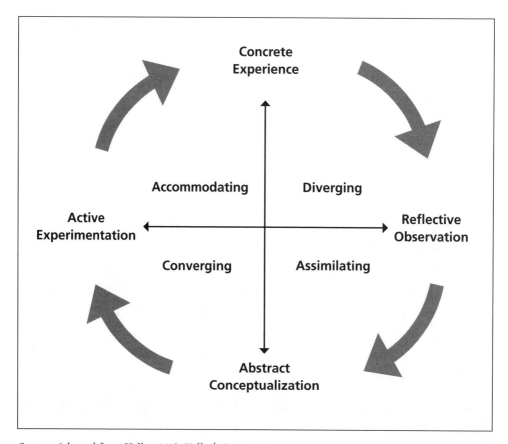

Source: Adapted from Kolb, 1984; Kolb & Fry, 1975.

Figure 6.1: Kolb and Fry's learning styles.

The learning style inventory can be used for new teachers before they begin professional learning so leaders can determine how teachers learn best. This helps with
preparation and planning and makes professional learning more relevant.

CAL Theory

Characteristics of Adult Learners (CAL) Theory states that when it comes to adult learning, there are two characteristics to consider: (1) personal characteristics and (2) situational characteristics (Cross, 1981). Personal characteristics include factors such as aging, life phases, and development phases, which all can influence learning. For example, with aging, sensory skills can begin to deteriorate (eyesight, hearing, and so on), but intelligence, such as reasoning and vocabulary, actually increases.

Life phases and *development phases* refer to where adults are in their life. For example, some are young and single, others could be new parents, and some could have children who are grown. These personal characteristics make up stages adults go through and have a significant impact on their learning.

Situational characteristics refer to the learning situation. For instance, is the learning that the adult is engaged in part-time or full-time? Is the learning voluntary or mandatory? In addition, the logistics of the learning also make an impact on adult learning—for example, the schedule or location of the learning.

The implication of CAL theory is that when teaching adults, leaders must plan for their constantly changing stages. Therefore, leaders should apply different learning strategies with adults based on the unique stage adults are in during their lives at that time. This is not easy to do; but think about how we expect teachers to differentiate lessons with their students. This is very similar to that expectation. How can you plan your professional development so that you keep your audience in mind in terms of where they are in their lives and any other unique factors about them?

Transformational Learning Theory

Jack Mezirow (1978) conducted a study involving eighty-three women who went back to college after having been on a long hiatus from school. He conducted in-depth interviews with each of them and concluded their success (or lack of success) was dependent on their perspective transformation. Mezirow (1978) outlines the following ten stages of transformational learning that allow for that perspective transformation to occur.

1. A disorienting dilemma (an experience that does not fit with the learner's experiences)

2. A self-examination with feelings of guilt or shame

3. A critical assessment of epistemic, sociocultural, or psychic assumptions

4. Recognition that one's discontent and the process of transformation are shared and that others have negotiated a similar change

5. Exploration of options for new roles, relationships, and actions

6. Planning a course of action

7. Acquisition of knowledge and skills for implementing one's plan

8. Provisional trying of new roles

9. Building of competence and self-confidence in new roles and relationships

10. A reintegration into one's life on the basis of conditions dictated by one's perspective

In essence, the transformational learning theory states an adult's personal experience plays a significant role in the entire learning process. These personal experiences create *meaning schemes*, defined as adult learners giving their own meaning to information based on their individual experiences. Specifically, meaning schemes are "made up of specific knowledge, beliefs, value judgments, and feelings that constitute interpretations of experience" (Mezirow, 1991, pp. 5–6).

A theory provides a generalized explanation of how something works. We have explored theories on adult learning. What generalizations, based on the research, have been made about adult learning? And, more importantly, what does that mean for school leaders as they create professional development opportunities for teachers in their buildings?

Ineffective Professional Development

Of course, districts and schools offer professional development to teachers all the time. Douglas B. Reeves (2010) states that "more than 90 percent of public school teachers participate in workshops, conferences, and training sessions" (p. 24). The question is not whether schools are providing professional development; rather, the question is how effective is it? Much has been written about the ineffectiveness of professional development (Darling-Hammond et al., 2017; Jayaram, Moffit, & Scott, 2012; Wei, Darling-Hammond, Andree, Richardson, & Orphanos, 2009). Principals and district leaders need to have an understanding of what factors lead to ineffective professional development. We discuss five of those factors here.

No Implementation Support

Most of the time school leaders have good intentions when providing professional development. They do research and then give new teachers lots of great information and ideas, but then teachers are set free to do what they will with the information. There is no guidance for implementation or next steps. This is where the breakdown often happens, when implementation doesn't go as expected. Every classroom is different and filled with students who have differing needs, so implementation will not be the same in all circumstances. This is where the support needs to be; how do teachers actually take what they learn in professional development sessions and then apply it to their classrooms? This is challenging for new teachers because they lack the experience to know how to apply their new learning in the classroom. In addition, think about how overwhelming all the necessary learning can be for a new role. Whether it's you first year teaching or your first year as a principal, there is a huge learning curve just for the job itself; trying to implement everything can be difficult, especially if no support is provided for implementation.

Once and Done

Some professional development comes in a "once and done" format. This is when teachers receive training on a topic, and because they attended one workshop, leaders assume they have been trained, and therefore are fully competent. However, it is well known that some of the best teaching strategies include repetition. Bruce Joyce and Beverly Showers (2002) state that you need to practice a new teaching strategy or skill at least twenty times before a teacher can master it and therefore has truly learned it. The more something is repeated, the more likely people are to learn it. As Darling-Hammond et al. (2017) explain:

> Effective professional development provides teachers with adequate time to learn, practice, implement, and reflect upon new strategies that facilitate changes in their practice. As a result, strong PD initiatives typically engage teachers in learning over weeks, months, or even academic years, rather than in short, one-off workshops. (p. 4)

Unfortunately, this is not how most leaders handle professional development for teachers. Instead, leaders bombard teachers with one-time professional learning and assume teachers learned it. Again, let's think about the impact this could have on a brand-new teacher. The learning curve of the job already is so steep. How is a new teacher supposed to sort through all the new learning and implement everything in his or her first year?

Not Useful or Relevant

Ineffective professional development can also be a result of it not being useful or relevant to teachers. Leaders must know their audience and its needs. For example, the professional development new teachers need could be very different from what veteran teachers or those who have been teaching for two to five years require. For example, a new teacher may need training on basic school operations, such as how to enter grades or how to use specific programs unique to the school or district that veteran teachers have already mastered. New teachers may need training on the school's or district's community, their history, their challenges, their successes, and so on. Veteran teachers may need professional development on new technologies or new best practices. Professional development should always be relevant. The best way to ensure that is by asking teachers what they want or need to learn. In addition, think about what new teachers in your building or district have needed in the past because what you know new teachers need in terms of professional development may be different than what new teachers themselves think they need. Both perspectives are important: what new teachers want and what you think they need.

Poor Quality Training

Who is facilitating or leading the training? This is sometimes a delicate issue; however, who is delivering the professional development in critical to the success of the training. Is he or she knowledgeable and have credibility with the training material? Is the trainer engaging or is he or she boring? The trainer is not only teaching new teachers but also modeling what effective teaching looks like. Take time to think through who will deliver the professional development to your teachers. If training is happening inside the school, sometimes the best presenters are the rock star teachers, but this is not always the case. Consider using an application process with veteran teachers to preview how they would structure professional development to new teachers. (See the reproducible "Teacher Presenter Application" on page 153 at the end of the chapter.)

Lacking Variety

Sometimes professional development can lack variety, which makes it ineffective. If every professional development opportunity you offer your new teachers is in the same format, it can get redundant, boring, and ineffective. Mix it up! Sometimes a sit-and-get session may be what new teachers need, but other times professional development in a collaborative setting is more beneficial. Trainers should use a variety of teaching strategies during professional development, just like when teaching lessons to students.

Also consider what training you are offering from year to year. Is it the same? Imagine teachers teaching the exact same lesson to the same students from year to year. Kartik Jayaram, Andy Moffit, and Doug Scott (2012) point out that this is not uncommon:

> Many systems invest significant sums in PD programs but do so as a habit, tending to offer the same set of training courses each year without regard for how they might fit into a comprehensive program or how effective they are. (p. 1)

Finally, we recommend always seeking input from new teachers on how the professional development experience can be improved. (See the reproducible "Professional Development Survey" on page 154 at the end of the chapter.) But at the same time, remember the purpose of professional development is to increase the teachers' capacity to teach effectively, so ultimately all students are learning at high levels.

Strategies for Effective Professional Development

Most professional development is ineffective because it neither changes teaching practices nor improves student learning (Gulamhussein, 2013; Jayaram et al., 2012). We offer the following strategies for effective professional development.

Keep It Simple

A key characteristic of great teaching is the ability to explain complex information in a simple manner. Leaders must make sure that they do not focus on too many initiatives and instead provide a sustained focus on a few key instructional priorities. For example, think of a time when a district or school provided professional development on a variety of topics, such as the following.

- Writing quality assessment questions
- Communicating with parents
- Differentiating in the classroom
- Personalizing learning
- Using social-emotional learning
- Using backward design
- Writing learning targets
- Analyzing data
- Grading

The list can go on and on. All the topics are extremely important and worthy of training; however, it's too much! School leaders cannot just throw everything at teachers in the name of professional development. Professional development isn't about implementing whatever "the big thing" is for that year. There needs to be a focus for professional development to turn into action. So by being simple, we are suggesting you pick one big theme for each year and align your professional development to that theme.

Remain Content Focused

Professional development is best delivered in the context of teachers' subject area. Regardless of whether teachers are working with coaches, teammates, or other professionals, teachers need to be working with the content they teach (Darling-Hammond et al., 2017). What this means is that professional development should focus on a variety of teaching strategies within that specific content area. For example, if you are providing training to teachers on writing quality assessment questions, then tailor that training to mathematics teachers by providing mathematics-specific examples. Then tailor it for the social studies teachers by providing social studies–specific examples. This will help support teachers while they are implementing their new learning within their classrooms because it is relevant to the content they teach.

Use Active Learning

One of the best strategies to develop teacher learning is by using active learning, which engages teachers directly in designing and trying out teaching strategies, providing them with the opportunity to engage in the same style of learning they are designing for their students. "Active learning, in sharp contrast to sit-and-listen lectures, engages educators using authentic artifacts, interactive activities, and other strategies to provide deeply embedded, highly contextualized professional learning" (Darling-Hammond et al., 2017, p. 7). If teachers actively learn, then they can take that strategy back to the classroom with an understanding of how to implement it effectively. With this strategy, teachers are learning by doing.

Provide Implementation Support

Teachers don't typically struggle with learning new approaches to teaching; rather, they struggle with implementing them (Fuller, 2001). Traditional professional development is ineffective because there is no ongoing support with the implementation. As mentioned earlier, studies have shown it takes, on average, twenty separate instances of practice before a teacher has mastered a new skill, with that number increasing along with the complexity of the skill (Joyce & Showers, 2002). Therefore, professional development that does not provide implementation support and is not sustained, focused, and ongoing will most often fail to affect teacher behavior.

The Center for Public Education published a report by Allison Gulamhussein (2013) in which she references studies that show that effective professional development programs require anywhere from fifty to eighty hours of instruction, practice, and coaching before teachers arrive at mastery. "It turns out teachers' greatest challenge comes when they attempt to implement newly learned methods into the classroom" (Gulamhussein, 2013, p. 10). If leaders want real changes in teaching practice, they have to provide ample and ongoing support during implementation.

Use Models of Effective Practice

Professional development should help teachers understand and see what best practice looks like. Gulamhussein (2013) explains:

> For example, instead of hearing about inquiry learning in science, a
> master teacher might teach a science class using inquiry methodol-
> ogy while being observed by a teacher who is learning this skill. In

this way, teachers can see how the method is used successfully in a class of real students. (p. 17)

These models of effective practice include clarifying purpose and learning goals; facilitating engaging classroom discussions; providing consistent descriptive feedback; creating and implementing formative assessments to measure student progress on skills, plan for interventions, and plan for extending learning; and working with students on executive function skills such as organization, planning, and monitoring their own work.

Use Coaching

Coaching is highly effective for helping teachers implement a new skill. In coaching, teachers work with a master educator before, during, and after a lesson, getting feedback on their implementation of a newly learned teaching skill. In the early 1980s, Showers and Joyce (1996) confirmed their hypothesis that "coaching, following initial training would result in much greater transfer than would training alone" (p. 13). From their extensive studies and research, the authors conclude that coaching is by far the best professional development element that will most likely result in teachers transferring their new learning into practice (Joyce & Showers, 2002). Coaching, they find, is even more effective than practice.

Require Collaboration, Reflection, and Feedback

Job-embedded collaboration, reflection, and feedback are essential to effective professional development, which means school leaders must create time in teachers' schedules for collaboration and reflection and provide teams with feedback on their progress; however, it is important that collaboration focuses on specific priorities related to the professional development. For example, allow teachers to see each other teaching. Specifically, imagine a collaborative team teaching the same lesson, and each lesson is recorded. Then, during a collaborative meeting, teachers take turns watching each of the videos as they get to see how each team member taught that same lesson. During this time, teachers collaborate, reflect, and provide each other with feedback (Loewus, 2017).

In PLCs, teachers work interdependently in grade-level or subject-area teams to focus on a cycle of inquiry that answers four critical questions (DuFour et al., 2016): (1) What do we want students to know and be able to do? (2) How do we know when they have learned it? (3) What do we do when they haven't learned it?

and (4) What do we do when they have already learned it? Teams work together to determine learning targets, create common formative assessments, and reflect on results and data to determine what interventions and extensions students may require. These collaborative teams are the perfect place for teachers to apply professional learning from professional development opportunities. When the structures and processes are already in place for collaboration to occur, then teams can easily take the next step of reflecting and providing feedback in order to grow as professionals. That is the essence of PLCs: How can teachers reflect on their practice collaboratively and then improve it? For example, a group of teachers might take a training to learn to use the electronic platform Kahoot! (https://kahoot.it) to get immediate feedback from students. The team first plans how they will use Kahoot! in the lesson (holding each other accountable for trying the new learning). After implementing the platform, they examine the data to determine if the assessment strategy was effective (reflecting on the new learning after implementing it). The PLC process allows teacher teams to grow as professionals, which is what professional learning is about.

Implement "Think Tanks"

Our district has developed a teacher-to-teacher staff development activity called "think tanks." Twice a year, once during the school year and once at the end of the year, the district provides the opportunity for staff to share their best practices in a two-day institute format. Basically, in a think tank, teachers come together to learn from each other. It's another form of collaboration, but what makes it different is that anyone can attend—not just the teams of teachers teaching the same grade level or content area. Depending on the collaborative professional learning you are designing, your think tank can meet more often than twice a year. Following are some collaborative professional learning activities (Blackburn & Williamson, 2015) that you can implement through a think tank.

- **Book study:** Teachers read a book and then come together to discuss the implications of what they read for their teaching practice.

- **Analysis of student work:** Teachers come together to analyze student work to collaborate on how their teaching practices influence student learning.

- **Learning walks:** Teachers come together to walk different classrooms and collaborate on what they learned from one another's observations.

- **Lesson study:** Teachers come together to observe each other's lessons and then provide feedback so everyone learns how they can do better.

- **Charrette:** Teachers come together to discuss issues and share solutions.

Look Ahead

School leaders must make a deliberate effort to support teacher professional development for research-based best instructional practices through organized training, coaching, peer collaboration, and active learning. Ultimately, the best professional development occurs when teachers learn and grow together. A PLC is the best foundation for professional learning because collaborative teams are set up for a cycle of continuous inquiry that makes implementing new learning, measuring it, reflecting on results, and making changes as needed to reach intended results.

Next Steps

"Teacher Presenter Application" (page 153) is an example of an application veteran teachers can use to apply to provide professional development to new teachers.

"Professional Development Survey" (page 154) is an example of a survey leaders can give to new teachers after they participate in professional development to get their feedback to improve the next professional development experience.

REFLECTION QUESTIONS

1. What does your current professional development program look like, both for new teachers and veteran staff? After reading this chapter, what aspect or aspects of your program will you change?

2. This chapter reviewed some reasons why professional development can be ineffective. Which reason resonates with you the most? How can you minimize its impact to ensure effective professional development in your school?

3. What information do you use to determine professional development for the year?

4. How do you individualize or personalize professional development?

Teacher Presenter Application

Thank you for your interest in facilitating a professional development opportunity for our school or district. Please take some time to answer the following questions so we can best assess your fit in our school's or district's professional development plan.

1. In what area or topic could you facilitate professional development? What makes you an expert in that area?

2. What engaging strategies will you use in your professional development session with new teachers?

3. What strategies or support will you provide after the professional development session is over?

4. How will you measure the success of your professional development session?

REPRODUCIBLE

Professional Development Survey

Thank you for participating in today's professional development session. Please take a few minutes to give us feedback to ensure we can continue to improve future professional development sessions with our teachers.

1. What aspect of today's professional development did you enjoy the most?

2. What was least valuable to you today?

3. How will you incorporate today's learning into your classroom?

4. What feedback do you have for the presenter?

Building Your Building © 2020 Solution Tree Press • SolutionTree.com
Visit **go.SolutionTree.com/leadership** to download this free reproducible.

Afterword

As we stated in our introduction, hiring and retaining great teachers is a huge investment not only for monetary reasons but also for the well-being of our most important commodities, our students. So yes, when we hire teachers, we are making million-dollar decisions. These decisions are so important we must ensure we do everything in our power to hire the right person for every job. We must build our building with the greatest materials to construct the most secure foundation possible.

Hiring great teachers has never been easy, and with the pool of teachers declining (Sutcher et al., 2016), it has become even more challenging for school leaders. With an expected increase in the student population of 20 percent through 2025 (Sutcher et al., 2016), both hiring and retaining teachers will be critical. The U.S. Department of Education's National Center for Education Statistics (2019) reports that high school graduation reached an all-time high with 85 percent of students graduating high school in the 2016–2017 school year. To continue that trend, school leaders must retain the great teachers they hire.

We believe that one of the most important things school leaders can do is to implement PLCs in which there is an intense focus on learning for all, a collaborative culture, and a focus on results. New teachers will thrive in this environment, and experienced teachers will want to remain throughout their teaching careers.

This book focuses on giving school leaders the knowledge and tools to effectively hire and retain great teachers. These decisions are big-money decisions, but most importantly, they are decisions that affect students not just while in the classroom, but well into the future as citizens of the world.

References and Resources

Aberdeen Group. (2013). *The power of employee recognition.* Accessed at http://
go.globoforce.com/rs/globoforce/images/AberdeenReportNovember2013.pdf on
December 21, 2018.

Aguilar, E. (2017, July 31). What's the difference between coaching and mentoring?
[Blog post]. *Education Week.* Accessed at http://blogs.edweek.org/teachers/coaching
_teachers/2017/07/whats_the_difference_between_c.html on July 10, 2019.

Alliance for Excellent Education. (2014). *The high cost of high school dropouts: The
economic case for reducing the high school dropout rate.* Accessed at https://all4ed
.org/take-action/action-academy/the-economic-case-for-reducing-the-high-school
-dropout-rate on December 21, 2018.

Almy, S., & Tooley, M. (2012). *Building and sustaining talent: Creating conditions in
high-poverty schools that support effective teaching and learning.* Washington, DC:
Education Trust.

American Association of School Personnel Administrators. (n.d.). *Principal/assistant
principal interview questions.* Accessed at https://aaspa.org/principalassistant
-principal-interview-questions on December 21, 2018.

American Institute of Stress. (n.d.). *Stress effects.* Accessed at https://www.stress.org
/stress-effects on July 15, 2019.

American Psychological Association. (2017, May 24). *Change at work linked to
employee stress, distrust and intent to quit, new survey finds* [Press release]. Accessed
at www.apa.org/news/press/releases/2017/05/employee-stress.aspx on December
21, 2018.

American Psychological Association's Center for Organizational Excellence. (2014).
Employee recognition survey. Washington, DC: Author.

American School Counselor Association. (n.d.). *Possible interview questions for school
counselors.* Accessed at www.schoolcounselor.org/administrators/interviewing
-school-counselors on December 21, 2018.

Andrews, H. A. (2011). Supporting quality teachers with recognition. *Australian
Journal of Teacher Education, 36*(12), 59–70.

Angelle, P. S. (2006). Instructional leadership and monitoring: Increasing teacher intent to stay through socialization. *NASSP Bulletin, 90*(4), 318–334.

Ball, D. L. (1996). Teacher learning and the mathematics reforms: What we think we know and what we need to learn. *Phi Delta Kappan, 77*(7), 500–508.

Barraza-Lyons, K., & Daughtrey, A. (2011). *The California science project teacher retention initiative: A final report.* Carrboro, NC: Center for Teaching Quality.

Behrman, E. (2017). *Many Harrisburg teachers resign over student violence.* Accessed at www.post-gazette.com/news/education/2017/11/22/Harrisburg-teachers-union-resign-student-violence-classroom-school-district-discipline/stories/201711220161 on May 22, 2019.

Bersin & Associates. (2012). *The state of employee recognition in 2012.* Accessed at https://google.com/url?sa=t&rct=j&q=&esrc=s&source=web&cd=1&ved=2ahUKEwjJ3MuQp_DgAhXNqYMKHRy6DP4QFjAAegQIARAC&url=https%3A%2F%2Fwww.hr.com%2Fen%3Fs%3D1Rj0W6IrJIGiTIKO%26t%3D%2FdocumentManager%2Fsfdoc.file.supply%26fileID%3D1355866281308&usg=AOvVaw1dgS2zNbWrHXnpsCsKLbG2 on December 21, 2018.

Blackburn, B., & Williamson, R. (2015). *Five tools for collaborative professional development.* Accessed at http://wsascd.org/wp-content/uploads/3-Five-Tools-for-Collaborative-Professional-Development1.pdf on July 9, 2019.

Blanchard, K. (2019). *Leading at a higher level: Blanchard on leadership and creating high performing organizations* (3rd ed.). Upper Saddle River, NJ: Pearson Education.

Bligh, J. (1999). Mentoring: An invisible support network. *Medical Education, 33*(1), 2–3.

Boogren, T. H. (2015). *Supporting beginning teachers.* Bloomington, IN: Marzano Resources.

Bower, D., Diehr, S., Morzinski, J., & Simpson, D. (1999). *Mentoring guidebook for academic physicians* (2nd ed.). Milwaukee, WI: Center for Ambulatory Teaching Excellence, Department of Family and Community Medicine, Medical College of Wisconsin.

Branham, L. (2005). *The 7 hidden reasons employees leave: How to recognize the subtle signs and act before it's too late.* New York: American Management Association.

Breslow, J. M. (2012). By the numbers: Dropping out of high school. *Frontline.* Accessed at www.pbs.org/wgbh/pages/frontline/education/dropout-nation/by-the-numbers-dropping-out-of-high-school on December 21, 2018.

Brill, S., & McCartney, A. (2008). Stopping the revolving door: Increasing teacher retention. *Politics & Policy, 36*(5), 750–774.

Brock, B. L., & Grady, M. L. (2001). *From first-year to first-rate: Principals guiding beginning teachers* (2nd ed.). Thousand Oaks, CA: Sage.

Brown, T. (2016, June 6). *Did you come to school today ready to learn? Communicating high expectations.* PLC Institute, Las Vegas, Nevada, June 6–8, 2016.

Brun, J.-P., & Dugas, N. (2008). An analysis of employee recognition: Perspectives on human resources practices. *International Journal of Human Resource Management, 19*(4), 716–730.

Carr, P., & Walton, G. (2014). Cues of working together fuel intrinsic motivation. *Journal of Experimental Social Psychology, 53,* 169–184.

Christie, M., Carey, M., Robertson, A., & Grainger, P. (2015). Putting transformative learning theory into practice. *Australian Journal of Adult Learning, 55*(1), 9–30.

Clement, M. C. (2013). Teachers hiring teachers. *Educational Leadership, 71*(2).

Cohen, H. (2011). *72 marketing definitions.* Accessed at www.HeidiCohen.com /marketing-definition on May 22, 2019.

Conzemius, A. E., & O'Neill, J. (2014). *The handbook for SMART school teams: Revitalizing best practices for collaboration* (2nd ed.). Bloomington, IN: Solution Tree Press.

Cornelius-White, J. (2007). Learner-centered teacher-student relationships are effective: A meta-analysis. *Review of Educational Research, 77*(1), 113–143.

Costa, A. L., & Kallick, B. (Eds.). (2008). *Learning and leading with habits of mind: 16 essential characteristics for success.* Alexandria, VA: Association for Supervision and Curriculum Development.

Cross, K. P. (1981). *Adults as learners.* San Francisco: Jossey-Bass.

Darling-Hammond, L. (2003). Keeping good teachers: Why it matters, what leaders can do. *Educational Leadership, 60*(8), 6–13.

Darling-Hammond, L., Hyler, M. E., & Gardner, M. (2017). *Effective teacher professional development.* Palo Alto, CA: Learning Policy Institute.

Davies, R. (2001). How to boost staff retention. *People Management, 7*(8), 54–56.

Doll, J. J., Eslami, Z., & Walters, L. (2013). Understanding why students drop out of high school, according to their own reports: Are they pushed or pulled, or do they fall out? A comparative analysis of seven nationally representative studies. *SAGE Open, 3*(4).

Douglas, E. (2012). *Promote internally or hire externally?* Accessed at http://blogs .edweek.org/topschooljobs/k-12_talent_manager/2012/06/promote_internally _or_hire_externally.html on July 25, 2019.

Downey, M. (2015). *Why are teachers leaving? Concerns over school safety and consistent enforcement of discipline.* Accessed at www.ajc.com/blog/get-schooled/why-are -teachers-leaving-concerns-over-school-safety-and-consistent-enforcement -disciplinc/uL8KpspC8YGuF9fXlShbfO on May 22, 2019.

DuFour, R. (2004). What is a professional learning community? *Educational Leadership, 61*(8), 6–11.

DuFour, R. (2009, May 26). *Is this candidate a good fit for a PLC?* [Blog post]. Accessed at www.allthingsplc.info/blog/view/51/is-this-candidate-a-good-fit-for-a-plc on December 21, 2018.

DuFour, R., DuFour, R., & Eaker, R. (2008). *Revisiting Professional Learning Communities at Work: New insights for improving schools.* Bloomington, IN: Solution Tree Press.

DuFour, R., DuFour, R., Eaker, R., Many, T. W., & Mattos, M. (2016). *Learning by doing: A handbook for Professional Learning Communities at Work* (3rd ed.). Bloomington, IN: Solution Tree Press.

DuFour, R., & Fullan, M. (2013). *Cultures built to last: Systemic PLCs at Work.* Bloomington, IN: Solution Tree Press.

DuFour, R., & Marzano, R. J. (2011). *Leaders of learning: How district, school, and classroom leaders improve student achievement.* Bloomington, IN: Solution Tree Press.

Douglas, K. (2012). *Exploring growth mindset for students and teachers.* Washington, DC: Center for Inspired Teaching.

Eaker, R., & Keating, J. (2015). *Kid by kid, skill by skill: Teaching in a Professional Learning Community at Work.* Bloomington, IN: Solution Tree Press.

Eberhard, J., Reinhardt-Mondragon, P., & Stottlemyer, B. (2000). *Strategies for new teacher retention: Creating a climate of authentic professional development for teachers with three or less years of experience.* Corpus Christi, TX: Texas A&M University, South Texas Research and Development Center.

Eby, L. T., Allen, T. D., Evans, S. C., Ng, T., & DuBois, D. L. (2008). Does mentoring matter? A multidisciplinary meta-analysis comparing mentored and non-mentored individuals. *Journal of Vocational Behavior, 72*(2), 254–267.

Education World. (2015). *Principals offer 30 ways to fight stress.* Accessed at www .educationworld.com/a_admin/admin/admin394.shtml on May 22, 2019.

Eichholz, T. (2017). *New teachers: How to talk to parents.* Accessed at www.edutopia .org/article/new-teachers-how-talk-parents-terri-eichholz on May 22, 2019.

Erkens, C., & Twadell, E. (2012). *Leading by design: An action framework for PLC at Work leaders.* Bloomington, IN: Solution Tree Press.

Feldman, D. C. (1999). Toxic mentors or toxic protégés? A critical re-examination of dysfunctional mentoring. *Human Resource Management Review, 9*(3), 247–278.

Ferriter, W. M., Graham, P., & Wight, M. (2013). *Making teamwork meaningful: Leading process-driven collaboration in a PLC at Work.* Bloomington, IN: Solution Tree Press.

Finley, T. (2013). *Rethinking whole class discussion.* Accessed at www.edutopia.org/blog /rethinking-whole-class-discussion-todd-finley on November 3, 2018.

Fisher, J. G. (2015). *Strategic reward and recognition: Improving employee performance through non-monetary incentives.* Philadelphia: Kogan Page.

Flavell, J. H. (1976). Metacognitive aspects of problem solving. In L. B. Resnick (Ed.), *The nature of intelligence* (pp. 231–236). Hillsdale, NJ: Erlbaum.

Fleming, S. M. (2014, September/October). Metacognition is the forgotten secret to success. *Scientific American Mind, 25*(5), 31–37.

Freeman, R. (2000). Faculty mentoring programmes. *Medical Education*, 34: 507–508.

Fullan, M. (2000). The three stories of education reform. *Phi Delta Kappan, 81*(8), 581–584.

Fuller, J. (2001). *Effective strategies for creating change within the educational system: A three-cycle action research study*. Paper presented at the Annual Meeting of the American Educational Research Association, Seattle, Washington.

Gillespie, R. (1991). *Manufacturing knowledge: A history of the Hawthorne experiments*. Cambridge, England: Cambridge University Press.

Goodreads. (n.d.). *Russell A. Barkley quotes*. Accessed at www.goodreads.com/author /quotes/215511.Russell_A_Barkley on July 23, 2019.

Gordon, G. (2004). Teacher retention starts with great principals. *Gallup*. Accessed at https://news.gallup.com/poll/10657/teacher-retention-starts-great-principals.aspx on January 4, 2019.

Grainge, C. (2002). Mentoring—supporting doctors at work and play. *BMJ Career Focus*, 324: S203.

Gray, L., & Taie, S. (2015). *Public school teacher attrition and mobility in the first five years: Results from the first through fifth waves of the 2007–08 Beginning Teacher Longitudinal Study* (NCES 2015–337). Washington, DC: National Center for Education Statistics. Accessed at https://nces.ed.gov/pubs2015/2015337.pdf on January 4, 2018.

Great. (n.d.). In *Merriam-Webster*. Accessed at https://www.merriam-webster.com /dictionary/great on July 2, 2019.

Gulamhussein, A. (2013). *Teaching the teachers: Effective professional development in an era of high stakes accountability*. Alexandria, VA: Center for Public Education.

Habits of mind. (n.d.). Accessed at https://chsvt.org/wdp/Habits_of_Mind.pdf on March 7, 2019.

Halper, L. (2017). *Mentee and mentor expectations*. Accessed at www.gavilan.edu/staff /mentors/roles.php on May 22, 2019.

Hargreaves, A., & Fink, D. (2004). The seven principles of sustainable leadership. *Educational Leadership, 61*(7), 8–13.

Hattie, J. A. C. (2003, October). *Teachers make a difference: What is the research evidence?* Paper presented at the Building Teacher Quality: What Does the Research Tell Us, Australian Council for Educational Research Conference, Melbourne, Australia. Accessed at https://research.acer.edu.au/cgi/viewcontent.cgi?article =1003&context=research_conference_2003 on January 4, 2019.

Hattie, J. A. C. (2009). *Visible learning: A synthesis of over 800 meta-analyses relating to achievement*. London: Routledge.

Hattie, J. A. C. (2012). *Visible learning for teachers: Maximizing impact on learning*. London: Routledge.

Herzberg, F., Mausner, B., & Snyderman, B. B. (1959). *The motivation to work* (2nd ed.). New York: Wiley.

Hodges, T. (2012). *Gallup's teacher applicant report and hiring date: TeacherInsight*. Accessed at https://google.com/url?sa=t&rct=j&q=&esrc=s&source=web&cd =2&ved=2ahUKEwj79vPm9_DgAhXH6YMKHbeuAvIQFjABegQICBAC&url =https%3A%2F%2Fwww.gallup.com%2Ffile%2Fservices%2F175979%2FGEC %2520HR%2520webinar%252010_30_13.pdf&usg=AOvVaw2AH5T_14w BGFa5lOk_5buG on March 7, 2019.

Hodges, T. (2015, May 22). *Don't wait until the school year ends to recognize teachers* [Blog post]. Accessed at http://news.gallup.com/opinion/gallup/183398/don-wait -until-school-year-end-recognize-teachers.aspx on January 4, 2019.

Hope, W. C. (1999). Principals' orientation and induction activities as factors in teacher retention. *The Clearing House: A Journal of Educational Strategies, Issues and Ideas, 73*(1), 54–56.

HR Council. (2018). [Employee recognition]. Accessed at http://hrcouncil.ca/hr -toolkit/keeping-people-employee-recognition.cfm on July 6, 2018.

Human Capital Institute. (2009). *The value and ROI in employee recognition: Linking recognition to improved job performance and increased business value—The current state and future needs*. Washington, DC: Author.

Ingersoll, R. M. (2001). Teacher turnover and teacher shortages: An organizational analysis. *American Educational Research Journal, 38*(3), 499–534.

Ingersoll, R. M., & Smith, T. M. (2004). Do teacher induction and mentoring matter? *NASSP Bulletin, 88*(638), 28–40.

Ingersoll, R. M., Smith, T., & Dunn, A. (2007, April). *Who gets quality induction?* Paper presented at the annual meeting of the American Educational Research Association, Chicago, Illinois.

Ingersoll, R. M., & Strong, M. (2011). The impact of induction and mentoring programs for beginning teachers: A critical review of the research. *Review of Educational Research, 81*(2), 201–233.

Jayaram, K., Moffit, A., & Scott, D. (2012). *Breaking the habit of ineffective professional development for teachers*. Accessed at www.mckinsey.com/industries/social-sector /our-insights/breaking-the-habit-of-ineffective-professional-development-for -teachers on January 7, 2019.

Johnson, S. M. (2006). *The workplace matters: Teacher quality, retention, and effectiveness*. Washington, DC: National Education Association. Accessed at http:// beta.nea.org/assets/docs/HE/mf_wcreport.pdf on January 7, 2018.

Johnson, W. B., & Andersen, G. (2009). How to make mentoring work. *Proceedings, 135*(4).

Johnson, W. B., Rose, G., & Schlosser, L. Z. (2007). Student-faculty mentoring: Theoretical and methodological issues. In T. D. Allen and L. T. Eby (Eds.), *The Blackwell handbook of mentoring: A multiple perspectives approach* (pp. 49–69). Oxford, England: Blackwell.

Joyce, B., & Showers, B. (2002). *Student achievement through staff development* (3rd ed.). Alexandria, VA: Association for Supervision and Curriculum Development.

Kanold, T. D. (2011). *The five disciplines of PLC leaders*. Bloomington, IN: Solution Tree Press.

Kardos, S. M., & Johnson, S. M. (2007). On their own and presumed expert: New teachers' experience with their colleagues. *Teachers College Record, 109*(9), 2083–2106.

King, A. (1993). From sage on the stage to guide on the side. *College Teaching, 41*(1), 30–35.

Knowles, M. S. (1973). *The adult learner: A neglected species*. Houston, TX: Gulf.

Kolb, D. (1984). *Experiential learning: Experience as the source of learning and development*. Englewood Cliffs, NJ: Prentice-Hall.

Kolb, D. A., & Fry, R. E. (1975). Towards an applied theory of experiential learning. In C. L. Cooper (Ed.), *Theories of group processes* (pp. 33–57). New York: Wiley.

Kossek, E. E., Pichler, S., Bodner T., & Hammer, L. B. (2011). Workplace social support and work-family conflict: A meta-analysis clarifying the influence of general and work-family-specific supervisor and organizational support. *Personnel Psychology, 64*(2), 289–313.

Kouzes, J. M., & Posner, B. Z. (2002). *The leadership challenge* (3rd ed.). San Francisco: Jossey-Bass.

Kullar, J. (2018). *Professional learning is more meaningful when done as a team*. Accessed at https://blogs.edweek.org/teachers/teaching_ahead/2018/01/teaching_ahead _post_1.html on May 22, 2019.

Levy, B. D., Katz, J. T., Wolf. M. A., Sillman, J. S., Handin, R. I., & Dzau, V. J. (2004). An initiative in mentoring to promote residents' and faculty members' careers. *Academic Medicine, 79*(9), 845–850.

Lewis, B. (n.d.). The value of self-reflection for success in teaching: Examining what failed in the past can lead to future triumphs. *ThoughtCo*. Accessed at www .thoughtco.com/self-reflection-for-success-in-teaching-2081942 on January 8, 2019.

Li, N., Zheng, X., Harris, T. B., Liu, X., & Kirkman, B. L. (2016). Recognizing "me" benefits "we": Investigating the positive spillover effects of formal individual recognition in teams. *Journal of Applied Psychology, 101*(7), 925–939.

Lipman, V. (2019). 36% of Employees say lack of recognition is top reason to leave their job. *Forbes*. Accessed at www.forbes.com/sites/victorlipman/2019/03/01/36 -of-employees-say-lack-of-recognition-is-top-reason-to-leave-their-job/#41b6d 2d945b4 on May 22, 2019.

Loewus, L. (2017). It's not how long you spend in PD, it's how much you grow. *Education Week*. Accessed at www.edweek.org/tm/articles/2017/12/06/its-not-how -long-you-spend-in.html on May 22, 2019.

Marzano, R. J. (2013). Art and science of teaching / asking questions—at four different levels. *Educational Leadership, 70*(5), 76–77.

Maslow, A. H. (1943). A theory of human motivation. *Psychological Review, 50*(4), 370–396.

McEwan, E. K. (2003). *10 Traits of highly effective principals: From good to great performance.* Thousand Oakes, CA: Corwin Press.

Meador, D. (n.d.). How principals can provide teacher support. *ThoughtCo.* Accessed at www.thoughtco.com/suggestions-for-principals-to-provide-teacher-support -3194528 on January 8, 2019.

Mentoring. (n.d.). In *Cambridge Dictionary.* Accessed at https://dictionary.cambridge .org/us/dictionary/english/mentoring on July 15, 2019.

Metacognition. (n.d.). In *Wikipedia.* Accessed at https://en.wikipedia.org/wiki /Metacognition on July 9, 2019.

Mezirow, J. (1978). *Education for perspective transformation: Women's re-entry programs in community colleges.* New York: Columbia University.

Mezirow, J. (1991). *Transformative dimensions of adult learning.* San Francisco: Jossey-Bass.

Mitchell, B. (2013). *Individual vs. team rewards: The 75/25 rule* [White paper]. Accessed at https://snowfly.com/wp-content/uploads/2016/08/Teams_V_indiv _Incentives_feb2013.pdf on January 7, 2019.

Mizell, H. (2010). *Why professional development matters.* Oxford, OH: Learning Forward. Accessed at https://learningforward.org/docs/default-source/pdf/why_pd _matters_web.pdf on January 8, 2019.

Morzinski, J. A., Diehr, S., Bower, D. J., & Simpson, D. E. (1996). A descriptive, cross-sectional study of formal mentoring for faculty. *Family Medicine, 28*(6), 434–438.

Murphy, S. (2014). *Top 5 ways to ditch top-down recognition for a more personal approach.* Accessed at http://switchandshift.com/5-ways-to-ditch-top-down -recognition-for-a-more-personal-approach on January 7, 2019.

Nagel, D. (2017). Report: Teachers spend up to $5,000 out of pocket on classroom supplies. *THE Journal.* Accessed at https://thejournal.com/articles/2017/08/08 /report-teachers-spend-up-to-5000-out-of-pocket-on-classroom-supplies.aspx on January 8, 2019.

Nagy, J., & Vilela, M. (n.d.). Chapter 15, Section 3: Providing support for staff and volunteers. *Community Tool Box.* Accessed at http://ctb.ku.edu/en/table-of -contents/leadership/effective-manager/staff-support/main on January 8, 2019.

National Center for Education Statistics. (2019). *Public high school graduation rates.* Accessed at https://nces.ed.gov/programs/coe/indicator_coi.asp on January 14, 2019.

National Commission on Teaching and America's Future. (2007). *Policy brief: The high cost of teacher turnover.* Washington, DC: Author. Accessed at https://nctaf.org /wp-content/uploads/NCTAFCostofTeacherTurnoverpolicybrief.pdf on December 21, 2018.

Navarro, J. (2008). *What every body is saying.* New York: Collins.

Nelson, B. (2012). *1501 ways to reward employees.* New York: Workman.

Nemanick, R. C. (2000). Comparing formal and informal mentors: Does type make a difference? *Academy of Management Executive, 14*(3), 136–138.

O'Donnell, M. (2014). 5 different ways to truly support your workplace. *TalentCulture.* Accessed at https://talentculture.com/5-different-ways-to-truly -support-your-workplace on January 14, 2019.

Ohio Department of Education. (2019). Resident educator program. Accessed at http:// education.ohio.gov/Topics/Teaching/Resident-Educator-Program on July 25, 2019.

Organisation for Economic Co-Operation and Development. (2009). *Creating effective teaching and learning environments: First results from TALIS.* Accessed at www.oecd .org/education/school/43023606.pdf on January 14, 2019.

Page, M. (n.d.). *The benefits of mentoring.* Accessed at www.michaelpage .co.uk/advice/management-advice/development-and-retention/benefits-mentoring on June 2, 2019.

Parker, W. D. (2017). *PMP: 076 Messaging matters–How to inspire teachers, motivate students and reach communities.* Accessed at https://williamdparker.com/2017/08/09 /pmp076-messaging-matters-how-to-inspire-teachers-motivate-students-and-reach -communities/ on July 15, 2019.

Pennsylvania Institute for Instructional Coaching. (n.d.). *What is an instructional coach?* Accessed at http://piic.pacoaching.org/index.php/piic-coaching/what-is-an -instructional-coach on December 21, 2018.

Perrachione, B. A., Rosser, V. J., & Petersen, G. J. (2008). Why do they stay? Elementary teachers' perceptions of job satisfaction and retention. *Professional Educator, 32*(2).

Podolsky, A., Kini, T., Bishop, J., & Darling-Hammond, L. (2016). Solving the teacher shortage: How to attract and retain excellent educators. *Learning Policy Institute.* Accessed at https://learningpolicyinstitute.org/product/solving-teacher -shortage on January 14, 2019.

Public Agenda. (2004). *Teaching interrupted: Do discipline policies in today's public schools foster the common good?* Accessed at https://files.eric.ed.gov/fulltext /ED485312.pdf on January 14, 2019.

Ragins, B. R., & Cotton, J. L. (1999). Mentor functions and outcomes: A comparison of men and women in formal and informal mentoring relationships. *Journal of Applied Psychology, 84*(4), 529–550.

Ragins, B. R., Cotton, J. L., & Miller, J. S. (2000). Marginal mentoring: The effects of type of mentor, quality of relationship, and program design on work and career attitudes. *Academy of Management Journal, 43*(6), 1177–1194.

RAND Education. (2012). *Teachers matter: Understanding teachers' impact on student achievement.* Accessed at www.rand.org/pubs/corporate_pubs/CP693z1-2012-09 .html on May 22, 2019.

Rath, T., & Clifton, D. O. (2004). *How full is your bucket? Positive strategies for work and life.* New York: Gallup Press.

Reeves, D. B. (2004). The case against the zero. *Phi Delta Kappan, 86*(4), 324–325.

Reeves, D. B. (2010). *Transforming professional development into student results.* Alexandria, VA: Association for Supervision and Curriculum Development.

Rentner, D. S., Kober, N., Frizzell, M., & Ferguson, M. (2016). *Listen to us: Teacher views and voices.* Accessed at https://files.eric.ed.gov/fulltext/ED568172.pdf on May 22, 2019.

Richards, J. (2007). How effective principals encourage their teachers. *Principal, 86*(3), 48–50.

Roche, G. R. (1979). Much ado about mentors. *Harvard Business Review, 57*(1), 14–20.

Ronfeldt, M., Farmer, S. O., McQueen, K., & Grissom, J. A. (2015). Teacher collaboration in instructional teams and student achievement. *American Educational Research Journal. 52*(3), 475–514.

Ross, J. (2011). Collaboration rules: Five reasons why collaboration matters now more than ever. *Forbes.* Accessed at www.forbes.com/sites/oreillymedia/2011/06/13 /collaboration-rules-five-reasons-why-collaboration-matters-now-more-than -ever/#69291d9c24c1on May 22, 2019.

Saunderson, R. (2004). Survey findings of the effectiveness of employee recognition in the public sector. *Public Personnel Management, 33*(3), 255–275.

Schmoker, M. (2003). First things first: Demystifying data analysis. *Educational Leadership, 60*(5), 22–24.

Schoolcounselor.com. (2019). *Interview questions.* Accessed at https://schoolcounselor .com/professional-development/interview-questions on July 25, 2019.

Self, J. (2018). *Classrooms in crisis: Why SC teachers are leaving in record numbers.* Accessed at www.thestate.com/news/local/education/article205569864.html on May 22, 2019.

Selye, H. (1974). *Stress without distress.* Philadelphia: Lippincott.

Serin, H. (2017). The role of passion in learning and teaching. *International Journal of Social Sciences and Educational Studies, 4*(1), 60–64.

Setty, R. (2015). 9 characteristics of a good mentoring relationship. *HuffPost.* Accessed at www.huffingtonpost.com/rajesh-setty/9-characteristics-of-a-good-mentoring -relationship_b_6674602.html on January 14, 2019.

Showers, B., & Joyce, B. (1996). The evolution of peer coaching. *Educational Leadership, 53*(6), 12–16.

Skinner, B. F. (1938). *The behavior of organisms: An experimental analysis.* New York: Appleton-Century.

Slezak, P. (2015, November 16). *The importance of reference checking* [Blog post]. Accessed at https://recruitloop.com/blog/recruiter-tips-the-importance-of-reference -checking on January 14, 2019.

Stansbury, K., & Zimmerman, J. (2000). *Lifelines to the classroom: Designing support for beginning teachers.* San Francisco: WestEd.

Stiggins, R. J. (2002). Assessment crisis: The absence of assessment *FOR* learning. *Phi Delta Kappan, 83*(10), 758–765.

Stiggins, R. J. (2008). *Assessment manifesto: A call for the development of balanced assessment systems.* Portland, OR: Educational Testing Service Assessment Training Institute.

Strauss, V. (2014, October 24). *Teacher spends two days as a student and is shocked at what she learns.* Accessed at https://www.washingtonpost.com/news/answer-sheet /wp/2014/10/24/teacher-spends-two-days-as-a-student-and-is-shocked-at-what -she-learned/?noredirect=on&utm_term=.fbfacfdb2cc8 on July 15, 2019.

Stronge, J. H., & Tucker, P. D. (2000). *Teacher evaluation and student achievement.* Washington, DC: National Education Association.

Sturt, D. (2015). The power of thank you. *Training Journal,* 57–59.

Sutcher, L., Darling-Hammond, L., & Carver-Thomas, D. (2016). *A coming crisis in teaching? Teacher supply, demand, and shortages in the U.S.* Palo Alto, CA: Learning Policy Institute.

Tavernise, S. (2012, February 9). Education gap grows between rich and poor, studies say. *New York Times.* Accessed at www.nytimes.com/2012/02/10/education /education-gap-grows-between-rich-and-poor-studies-show.html?pagewanted=all on January 14, 2019.

Teaching Tolerance. (2016). *Reframing classroom management: A toolkit for educators.* Accessed at www.tolerance.org/sites/default/files/TT_Reframing_Classroom _Managment_Handouts.pdf on May 22, 2019.

Terada, Y. (2019). Understanding a teacher's long-term impact. *Edutopia.* Accessed at www.edutopia.org/article/understanding-teachers-long-term-impact on May 22, 2019.

Terera, S. R., & Ngirande, H. (2014). The impact of rewards on job satisfaction and employee retention. *Mediterranean Journal of Social Sciences, 5*(1), 481–487.

Tooms, A., & Crowe, A. (2004, November/December). Hiring good teachers: The interview process. *Principal, 84*(2), 50–53.

U.S. Equal Employment Opportunity Commission. (n.d.). *Prohibited employment policies/practices.* Accessed at https://www.eeoc.gov//laws/practices/#recruitment on July 15, 2019.

Valet, V. (2019). *America's best employers by state.* Accessed at www.forbes.com/best -employers-by-state/#5fd490be487a on July 25, 2019.

Viadero, D. (2018). Teacher recruitment and retention: It's complicated. *Education Week.* Accessed at www.edweek.org/ew/articles/2018/01/24/teaching-shortages -many-answers-for-a-complex.html on January 14, 2019.

Ventrice, C. (2009). *Make their day! Employee recognition that works—Proven ways to boost morale, productivity, and profits* (2nd ed.). San Francisco: Berrett-Koehler.

Vescio, V., Ross, D., & Adams, A. (2008). A review of research on the impact of professional learning communities on teaching practice and student learning. *Teaching and Teacher Education, 24*(1), 80–91.

Vroom, V. H. (1964). *Work and motivation.* New York: Wiley.

Warren, F. (2018). 10 interview questions for a potential instructional coach. *Instructional Coach Academy.* Accessed at https://theinstructionalcoachacademy .com/index.php/2018/03/19/10-interview-questions-for-a-potential-instructional -coach on January 14, 2019.

Wei, R. C., Darling-Hammond, L., Andree, A., Richardson, N., & Orphanos, S. (2009). *Professional learning in the learning profession: A status report on teacher development in the U.S. and abroad.* Dallas, TX: National Staff Development Council.

Wingfield, B., & Berry, J. (2001). *Retaining your employees: Using respect, recognition, and rewards for positive results.* Menlo Park, CA: Crisp.

WorldatWork. (2013). *Trends in employee recognition.* Scottsdale, AZ: Author.

Zeichner, K. M., & Gore, J. M. (1990). Teacher socialization. In W. R. Houston (Ed.), *Handbook of research on teacher education* (pp. 329–348). New York: Macmillan.

Index

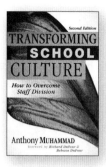

Transforming School Culture [Second Edition]
Anthony Muhammad
The second edition of this best-selling resource delivers powerful, new insight into the four types of educators and how to work with each group to create thriving schools. The book also includes Dr. Muhammad's latest research and a new chapter of frequently asked questions.
BKF793

The Beginning Teacher's Field Guide
Tina H. Boogren
The joys and pains of starting a teaching career often go undiscussed. This guide explores the personal side of teaching, offering crucial advice and support. The author details six phases every new teacher goes through and outlines classroom strategies and self-care practices.
BKF806

Take Time for You
Tina H. Boogren
The key to thriving as a human and an educator rests in self-care. With *Take Time for You*, you'll discover a clear path to well-being. The author offers manageable strategies, reflection questions, and surveys that will guide you in developing an individualized self-care plan.
BKF813

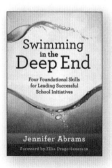

Swimming in the Deep End
Jennifer Abrams
Acquire the knowledge and resources necessary to lead successful change initiatives in schools. In *Swimming in the Deep End*, author Jennifer Abrams dives deep into the four foundational skills required of effective leadership and provides ample guidance for cultivating each.
BKF830

Solution Tree | Press

a division of

Solution Tree

Visit SolutionTree.com or call 800.733.6786 to order.

" Tremendous, tremendous, tremendous!

The speaker made me do some very deep internal reflection about the **PLC process** and the personal responsibility I have in making the school improvement process work **for ALL kids**. "

—Marc Rodriguez, teacher effectiveness coach,
Denver Public Schools, Colorado

PD Services

Our experts draw from decades of research and their own experiences to bring you practical strategies for building and sustaining a high-performing PLC. You can choose from a range of customizable services, from a one-day overview to a multiyear process.

Book your PLC PD today!
888.763.9045

Solution Tree